the Voice within the Wind

the Voice within the Wind

of Becoming and the Druid Way

Greywind

Grey House in the Woods

First published 2001

Published by
Grey House in the Woods
PO Box 8211
Girvan
Ayrshire
KA26 0WA
Scotland

ISBN 0 9540531 0 9

Set in 9 point Comic Sans MS and printed in Great Britain by ProPrint, Riverside Cottages, Old Great North Road, Stibbington, Cambridgeshire, PE8 6LR.

CONTENTS

ACKNOWLEDGEMENTS

It would be impossible to acknowledge all those whose influence has guided me to and through and blessed the making of this book. There have been many, in this world and in the Other. I thank them all from the depths of my being. May they continue to guide me. May I continue to be worthy of their trust.

I would, however, like to make particular mention of the following for the special roles they have played.

My wife, Barbara, whose deep rooted strength is a calm centre in a wild world and who gives of that strength and of her love unceasingly.

Gwynddydd and her twin brother Myrddin, keepers of my Grove.

Cydymeithion y Seren Arian, friends long since scattered into the forest, some now on their long journey - may your stars guide you well.

Charis, there at the beginning. The Grey Knight is still on his quest.

Julie, Beth, Maddy, Gael and Eileen - fellow travellers whose companionship is a sweet song of sustaining power.

My thanks, also, to Loreena McKennitt for the music.

Sketches for parts of this book have appeared in 'The Druids' Voice'.

Greywind
Clas Myrddin

for
Barbara

as the sun
you are the warmth and the light that nurtures my soul

as the moon
you cast light into the dark times of my heart

as the stars
you are a beacon that guides my spirit to the dawn

as the earth
you are the foundation of my life

as the sea
you are the ceaseless wonder that touches my shore

as the forest
you are the source of my wisdom

EARTH SONGS

1

listen until the machine runs down
you will have to listen long into the night
and where the earth is most blighted
you will have to listen with other ears
only listen

it will take practice
many days or many years
it will take patience and understanding
above all understanding
a supreme effort to come to see the machine
to come to know its ways
to learn to hear its grinding scream
to learn to hear it
one night
as it runs down

and in the special places
where its grip is still loose
in the special places you may have to create
in your head
you will hear

you will hear
a fragment of silence

first it will be a silence
that is an absence of noise
an absence of the grinding
an absence of the scream

it will become a silence
that is a repose
a freedom

and then
if you are not seduced to sleep
you will hear

you will hear
the song of the earth

2

sun above the landscape
rising in blazing splendour of birth
shining with life heat upon the earth
drawing the corn from the god mother's girth
high in the sky
bloated at sunset
pale in mist
seed of being
bringer of joy
to warm our blood
gift of father
listen
this is the song

wind across the hilltops
playing in eddies about the barrow
plying the stalks of sun ripe yarrow
whistling through the gap that is narrow
fresh from the sea
heavy with thunder
cold of snow
wing of cloud

movement of air
to kiss our blood
gift of the sky
listen
this is the song

earth beneath our brief feet
curving in hillside above the field
giving forth of its autumn yield
drawing life from the dead there concealed
turned by the plough
broken by frost
green in spring
womb of life
tomb of the dead
to feed our blood
gift of mother
listen
this is the song

water throughout all domains
falling in curtain that sweeps the land
running in courses on beds of sand
dancing ceaseless along the strand
warm in summer
stone hard in winter
blood of earth
air of fish
quencher of thirst
to cool our blood
gift of the cloud
listen
this is the song

3

to be born of the earth sweet mother of life
to know that i shall return to the rich darkness
and become one with she
who gave me my moment of self
i am her child and i love her

to stand as the world-tree embraced by all and all-embracing
with my roots deep and firm in the soil
my head in the high clouds
a life partly as the falling leaf
partly as the flying vapour

to produce and consume no more than i need
to take only what i can return
knowing the things which making me rich
will not make others poor
for there is no wealth but life

to refuse to worship at the shrine of the machine
and to make no sacrifice to it
to refuse any technology
which so arranges the world
that it can no longer be touched

to flow without contending as a river to the sea
a giver of life with ceaseless strength
that will wear down any barrier
in search of a way
that is not the constant way

to employ the power of truth and love
to wean from error by patience and sympathy
those who rape the earth and her children
those who by degrees
are committing the crime of matricide

to see things as they should be seen
to see them whole
for no thing is separate from another
all are but distinct facets
of a jewelled unity

to know the seasons of sister moon
and feel her tides in your blood
to know the days of father sun
and take joy
in the dance of the stars

to cherish our children and give them freedom
listen to their voices
to their hopes to their dreams
to the cries of those who starve
for they are the future

to find our place in nature
neither under nor over
that we may at last rest
and have time
to watch the grass grow

to hear the song of all living things
in the misted silence of dawn meadows
in the shadow of the turning world
to learn again our own song
and raise our voices in harmony

to walk the paths of the sleeping fay
and be touched by the dim echo
of their voice
and their wisdom
in the silence of the high places

to treasure the earth that is alive
and come to know all her names
to treat her as befits a mother
for she is life
and i am hers

OBSCURED BY CLOUDS

There may come a time in your life when the clouds part, moved by winds whose coming and purpose are beyond our knowing. They do have purpose. They will come.

When the clouds part, it will be given to you to see some of the details of what before had been uncertain forms in the obscuring mist.

The parting of the clouds may happen only once. The parting may be brief. No matter. The light that comes through will be enough. It will inform you. Memory of it will never be lost.

And listen, too, for within the convoluted music of the wind is a voice of subtle wisdom.

You may hear strange things, see distant stars, you may simply see and hear a little more of the landscape around you. Large or small, distant or near, it does not matter. It is all worthy of note.

In what ways you make sense of the detail revealed, in what ways the light and the voice inform you, in what ways the memory of this touches your self - all this depends on how you have prepared yourself for the moment.

Study the forms in the mist; come to know their shapes and movements. Know, too, what sort of thing is your goal. Know the ways of knowing. Then you may better understand what the light and the voice have revealed to you.

There are many ways of knowing. But if the slow presence of living wood is there in the light, with skyward reaching branches that listen to the wind that moves them, the way revealed is the Forest Way - born of a Celtic vision of a living world.

So, yet another book about Druids and the Druid Way? Yes, but no.

This is not a book about the Druid Way in the conventional sense. There are no ceremonies or rituals or workings herein. There are no initiations or exercises. Nor are there any revelations of arcana - there are no such secrets and there never have been.

Becoming Druid, taking to the Druid Way, does not depend on some hidden and closely guarded lore any more than it depends on surface manifestations. A Druid is inspired by the most essential, bright, open and accessible of sources. That the source has become obscured and that learning how to learn from it has been made difficult are expressions of the society in which we live rather than any obscurity inherent in Druidic thought and action.

To recognize the bright source, to come to terms with the things we learn from and experience in its presence, we need to think about and approach the world in a way different from that which has become the accepted norm. To achieve that involves a long and difficult journey.

It is a journey through the labyrinth to the very heart of our being, a journey that moves outward to touch the most distant star. It is a journey in which you may be guided by others, but which you must make for yourself. A journey in the real world, not in an abstract and partial world of symbols or the world of a humanity divorced from nature. For our forebears it was the natural and accepted way, just as it is for those who are truly Druid today.

This book aims, in part, through a series of questions and discussions of that Celtic vision to give some idea of how that metaphysic can be realized, won back from the dead hand of modern thought that has tried to steal it from our souls. It is, therefore, a book about magic - re-aligning the mind to work in concord with the universe and restore a balance that has been disturbed.

It is also a personal journey into the evolving spiritual and metaphysical aspects of that re-claimed perspective so that we all (myself included) might better hear the Voice, see the Light, and know the Truth.

Before starting that journey, there is an important point to consider. This is a book. In the past, Druids rarely wrote down their teachings. This is not to say they were illiterate. Many could read and write but, as part of a pattern of respect for the Goddess, they chose not to commit their wisdom to books. I do not claim that what follows constitutes wisdom, but this past reluctance is worth some thought.

Wisdom is not an abstract notion waiting to be plucked from some misty, distant and ancient realm of ideals by an adept of arcane methods. It is not contained in any book, guarded by zealous acolytes. Wisdom is of this world, dynamic and organic - a realization that all things are connected. It relates to being - we 'become' wise, but a book, no matter how erudite the content, is something we 'have'. It relates to time and place - blossoming in specific, concrete situations. And thus it relates to use, for if it is not applied it has neither meaning nor existence. Wisdom is, therefore, a predisposition of people to act and behave in certain right ways.

Wisdom is to understand what we know of the world that we might act rightly and for the good in the simplest way. If we know things poorly, improperly, or second hand, if we cannot see the connections between them, then we cannot ever come to understand them or act rightly.

We must, then, learn to know things properly. And this cannot be done solely by reading books and meditating on what we have read. There is a place for this, but we can only meditate on things that, ultimately, we derive from and are able to apply to a personal experience of the world. 'Do, and you understand' encapsulates this well.

If you tear wisdom out of people and pin it to the page it ceases to be wisdom. Rendering it as fixed symbols reduces it to nothing more than information. Unless this information is approached in the right spirit - knowing it for what it is, knowing the ways of reviving it and reintegrating it, knowing how alphabet literacy can work against the Goddess - it can become a dead weight that does not decay as it should to nourish new growth but, through its increasing irrelevance, becomes a deadly pollutant.

For those, like myself, who treasure books this is a difficult but truly vital point to accept. Books *are* important. They can be great teachers. But no matter how important they are, no matter how profound their message, we should always remember that books are simply one medium through which human beings can communicate. What they teach will reside within us, altering us and how we treat the world.

No book, especially one like this, is an end in itself. It is part of a cycle, part of a conversation to which you must contribute. Books fix words and ideas to make it easier to convey such conversations to many others. But, because the words are fixed on the page, we must not assume the ideas they convey to be immutable. Ideas are part of human experience. They evolve, have contact with the concrete world, and have relevance to our everyday lives.

Ultimately, the only worthwhile measure of what we have learned, of the wisdom we have derived from this, is in how we behave. Our behaviour as autonomous beings involves taking responsibility for what we are and what we do. That responsibility cannot be abrogated on the strength of something that has been read in a book and that may, in any case, have been misunderstood. Responsibility lies in conscious choice, in having control - which means acting from your *own* volition.

We live too much inside our heads in an abstract universe derived from a set of symbols on the page. It is important that we get out and do, for it is the actions of our lives that count, not the words in a book. The truly sacred is in the detail of our everyday lives, each act chosen for its rightness.

This book, then, is just a beginning. Re-aligning our metaphysical notions is vital, but only in so far as we then make use of that. You can learn many things about the Druid Way from books, but you cannot become Druid just by reading them. What you *can* learn about from a book is yourself; the most important thing you can then do, is apply what you have learned.

I have tried my best to speak the Truth. However, I have no monopoly on that, any more than I have a full understanding of what it is. My view is partial and I am fallible. There will, no doubt, be things herein that you find contentious. That is all to the good. What follows is offered as food for your thoughts (and we must surely feed our thoughts with as nutritious, varied, and healthy a diet as we offer our stomachs). And, through the questions I have raised and explored, I hope to have offered you an opportunity to clarify your own sense of direction.

Read the book. And when the book is finished, return to the world with a renewed vision. Then, gentle as your footsteps may already be upon the Earth, they will also be to some certain purpose - taking you closer to the Light.

WHERE THE JOURNEY BEGINS

Where to begin? As all journeys do - at the beginning. And with a journey of the spirit, it is you that are the beginning. That is quite straightforward. But, as with everything on this sort of journey, it is far from simple. For if the journey must begin from where you are, that means you must know where you are.

You might think it impossible for things to be otherwise, yet it is surprising how many do not. That is, they try to begin from a place they think they are, a place they have been told they are, or a place they believe they ought to be starting from. This is because they have not taken the time to prepare themselves - by being still and learning where they actually are.

All movement should start with stillness. Not a negative stillness - one in which all thought is directed toward the movement to come. Rather, it should be a stillness in which the soul, the spirit, can assess itself, place itself, prepare itself, and, most importantly, come to know itself. This is not just a spiritual necessity; it is plain common sense. If you do not know who or where you are, your journey is virtually impossible to plan.

It is, of course, of equal importance that you have some idea of where you want to go, what you want to become. Being too precise limits one's scope, introduces a rigidity that suppresses one's ability to develop and find the correct channel for one's development. On the other hand, too much vagueness means you will lack any sense of direction.

Striking a happy balance is one of the many lessons that is to be learned. That and the ability to recognize that goals we may once have set are no longer valid. Holding on tightly to what we want is extremely important, but so too, if the time comes, is letting go of it lightly. It is also important to recognize that the way we do things is as important as what we do. Begin the journey with stillness and the journey has begun.

These two points, the place you are and the place you want to be, help define the journey you must make. Indeed, the coming to know where one is and the formulation of where one wants to be are important elements of the journey. When you have settled these things, you generally find that you have made a good start to bridging the gap between.

There is little difference or distinction between learning where you are and knowing where you want to be. The two searches are merely facets of an approach towards a greater integration of the self. In learning where you are and what sort of person you are, you will inevitably come to know where it is you want to be. Deciding where you want to be helps to ascertain the current nature of your being.

Finding out where you are - that is, getting to know yourself - is not a static pastime. Indeed, it is highly dynamic for even if it occurs in a quiet room, sitting still and calm in a chair, it will change you in the most fundamental of ways. It will carry you on those first difficult steps toward your goal. In many senses, it is the whole of the journey.

At the same time, deciding where you want to be also invokes inner change, increasing the potential to flow from one state to the other. And, as with knowing where you are, knowing where you want to be is a search that should start from where you are. Understanding the nature of your being leads to an understanding of its potential.

Knowing yourself also means knowing your environment, material and spiritual, as you do not exist in isolation any more than what you are has come about in isolation. The environment of our being has helped create us and also determines the way in which we approach knowing ourselves. It also provides the means by which we move from where we are to where we want to be. This, the way of achieving our goals, is a third facet of the integration of our being.

The holistic and cyclical nature of the spiritual quest becomes apparent in all this. Knowing where you are means knowing where you want to be means knowing where you are. Knowing yourself means knowing what you want to be means knowing yourself.

Knowing the means by which this can be achieved means knowing ourselves means knowing the means by which this is to be achieved. Each is immanent in the others.

Whilst it is true that the closer you get to your ultimate goal, the more you realize that it is universal in its nature - the same as everyone else's ultimate goal - it is also the case that the ways of achieving that goal are, in their earlier stages, highly distinctive. And, having been instrumental in shaping us, those distinctive ways make it easier for each of us to start from where we are.

Identifying the two end-points of your quest, or the nature of the environment, is not sufficient in itself to carry out that quest. To begin with, those two points are mutable, changing as you explore. They are not fixed in time, space, or even within themselves. The moment you begin to define them and examine what you have defined, they take on new characteristics. And they will continue to do so.

Who you are, for example, changes the very second you decide to find out who you are. You have altered yourself by taking that step. And whereas you might be able to pinpoint that moment, all other moments are fluid because the goals become fluid. You may have a definite aim in mind, but it will soon become apparent that that, too, changes the very moment you take your first step toward it. Nor is what you have undertaken a linear exercise.

All things are connected and in a spiritual quest we must engage with them all. Which is why starting such a quest is so daunting and why your first steps are difficult and uncertain. Once you get into the way of things you begin to feel that you are simply going round in circles, returning always to the same problems and the same lessons. Eventually this resolves itself and you realize that the circle is also a spiral, that each cycle is also a progression - reflecting the basic nature of the universe.

So, why the Druid Way? Why not Christianity? Why not Buddhism? Why not any other one of the myriad ways that exist? In one sense, the answer has already been given. However, all such questions have many answers on many levels. Those not used to such complexity, those who do not have the patience to consider the many meanings, all too often simply see a single facet - that which most conforms to their own unconscious bias.

In essence, the answer lies in the material and spiritual environment in which we are raised and which, therefore, helps to shape our being. This is the starting from where you are. But it is also to do with an allied aspect - the ground that exists between the place that you are and the place you want to be. The environment that has already shaped you is also the environment through which you must travel when you begin your journey - the reason why we are each suited to a given Way.

This environment is not always obvious. It takes a very straight eye to see through the glittering veneer most people accept as the real world. Beneath that veneer, deep within each of us, lies the world that has shaped us over the millennia and which still affects much of what we think and do. The conflict between the way we have been shaped and the veneer to which we are supposed to conform causes a great deal of dis-ease.

Many who seek to bring the Light into their spirit do so because they feel displaced. They feel like they are on the wrong planet, in the wrong society or culture, in the wrong time. This feeling, they believe, derives from an environment to which they do not belong. They look outside themselves (as if everything is to be found 'out there'), they do not like what they see, and they blame the environment in which they live for all that is wrong with their lives.

This is especially true in what we might call - imprecisely, but for want of a better name - Contemporary Western Society. Anyone who looks at it closely will soon see that it is not a pretty prospect and many look elsewhere for a place in which they can feel at home. But what they have seen is not their true environment.

Contemporary Western Society is a bizarre construct of vested interests that has made a very effective job of subverting and hiding whatever has stood in its way during the short time in which it has developed. Our limited human perspective, however, means that we now know little else. It has become all too familiar. And familiarity breeds contempt - not for that with which we are familiar, but for that which our Society tells us is contemptible.

So it is that we are left with a sense that our native traditions and achievements are, for some reason, to be despised. If we are to believe this contrived picture, then prior to the civilizing influence of Rome, Britons were nothing more than savages. If a thing is to be culturally acceptable it has to be based in Greek or Latin thought, history or mythology. Antiquarians who have studied the Celtic and pre-Celtic past have always been considered eccentric, to put it politely.

The same picture is true when it comes to our spiritual heritage. Most people living in Britain assume this to be a Christian country. But it has never been that in more than a nominal sense - often enforced by a perverted form of teaching that has considered torture and execution as valid forms of proselytizing. A truly Satanic Church.

Seeing what the Church has done and continues to do to the teachings of the Christ, seekers after the Light have understandably looked elsewhere. Assuming Christianity to be the sole native option, they have sought beyond these islands and as far beyond the bounds of Christendom as they could go. As a result, it has to be the Far East or the transatlantic West before you have gone far enough to find something that is sufficiently exotic to suit the jaded spiritual palate.

That Contemporary Western Society has managed to subvert or hide so much of our genuine cultural and spiritual traditions does not mean they are not there to be found. They have survived to a very great degree. It simply makes the task of finding them much more difficult as one has first to overcome the deep-seated indoctrination to which we are all subjected. In one sense, this is a real service to the genuine seeker, but the distortion of reality has now reached dangerous proportions.

Even when people get beyond that initial barrier and find that there is something here on their own doorstep, many of them are disappointed by what they find. There are a number of reasons for this. It is difficult for anyone to be discriminating about what they discover because they are not properly trained. And when they find themselves confronted by a second glittering veneer they are just as confused as before. There are books in abundance to be read, self-styled gurus to follow, a plethora of systems for sale, orders and societies into which one can be initiated. So many promises - so little substance.

At this stage of the quest, the seeker has wandered into a playground, full of children playing. All is movement and brightness with so many wonderful new games to learn. It is a tantalizing and enchanting vista. One can become completely absorbed by all the games as well as the general etiquette and apparent vitality. So much so that one neglects the real purpose of being in a playground - which is to progress to the school just beyond.

There is a place in all our lives for the playground and its games. Indeed, we must all play before we can learn. And once the learning has begun, there is always a need for release and for fun, for re-creation. Even the wisest of sages will play. But we cannot stay in the playground forever if we wish to attain our goal.

The enchantment cast by the playground is no accident. It is a portrayal of our native spiritual tradition that is designed to attract and excite. The progenitors of this vision are manipulative self-publicists, the charlatans who inhabit the fringes. They sensationalize the tradition and portray themselves as masters of it (for it is mostly men). But all they are masters of is the playground, masters at disguising what the playground is.

Most of these jesters are harmless. Some are not. However, they all conspire in presenting a false world, one that is alive with supernatural forces and conflict, one in which there are great and dangerous quests, brooding heroes, outlandish folk, and the inevitable magician. This might be considered inoffensive, a bit of escapism. That is what the playground is for. But there is a deeper, insidious and dangerous message inherent in what transpires. It is that self is the centre of all, that self-improvement is the goal rather than the means to the goal.

This is most often done through irresponsible claims about magic. Magic is not about weird concoctions and potions, wild ceremonies, or any of the sick inventions of the medieval witch hunters. Nor is it something that can be used for personal advantage any more than it can be allowed to disturb the equilibrium of the universe. Attempts to perform magic in this way are acts of violence .

Magic is about discovering and coming to understand the patterns and balances that underlie all things. It is about working in concord with them in order to maintain or re-establish those patterns and balances. We all work magic of some form or another every day - using herbs to heal, gardening organically, preparing a meal. Those who devote their life to magic, learn to live their whole life in harmony with the natural order.

Anyone who truly seeks will ultimately be disappointed by what they find in the playground. The attractions soon pall. Some will find their way through to what is beyond - and it is well worth persisting. Sadly, all too many are driven away from their spiritual heritage. But it is not just that one's heritage is further hidden. If any continue with their quest, they are deprived of the chance of starting from where they are, they are deprived of a proper connection with the physical, cultural, psychological, and spiritual environment that originally shaped them.

Those who turn elsewhere generally look to the East. They do so because Eastern Ways have well documented histories, continuity, respectability, depth, and more than a hint of exoticism. What is more, they seem to be able to fulfil their claims, keep their promise of what they offer. By this same reckoning - albeit false - Western Ways do not. But that impression is arrived at because in the search for a specific Way, people have neglected to understand what any of these Ways actually are, where they lead, what they can do for the person. They can, of course, do nothing. They are not external forces to be tapped into and to be controlled for self-advantage. They are what we become. It is we who must act, we who must transform, we who are the Way.

This is, without any doubt, a simplistic account of the situation, but it is a fair representation of the popular conception. And it is on that perception of things that most people rely, as that is all they know. But those who look to the East for guidance, just as those who look to the sky, have missed what is to be had at our feet and at our fingertips in our own, familiar place.

It cannot be denied that there may be guidance in the sky or points east and west of where we are, any more than it can be denied that there are valuable lessons to be learned in and of these places. But all of that is devalued and lacks context if we ignore that to which, through ourselves, it is related, and that which gave us life and maintains us in it, both physically and spiritually.

No matter how hard we strive toward the Light, we start as creatures of this ground, this soil, this earth. We belong to Her, to this part of Her, and not She to us. If we cannot come to see our place with fresh eyes, if we do not understand the landscape we are to be guided through, we cannot properly follow the guidance.

This is not to argue that what is distinct should be made separate - something that is not, in any case, possible. We need a mix in order to provide vigour. We need those amongst us who know, understand, and follow other Ways as they provide us with a valuable perspective on our own Way - one that prevents insularity, one that aids in evolution. Besides, there will always be those who have started their search here and still find the need to move beyond those boundaries.

Important as these other Ways are, it is in the immensely rich and long-standing traditions of the pre-Celtic and ancestral Celtic peoples of these islands that our experience of the world is rooted. Much has been said in recent years to question whether there was in fact such a thing as a Celt or, if that, such a thing as a common Celtic vision. While it is true that there have been silly and extravagant claims made, the existence of the Celts and a Celtic metaphysic cannot simply be denied because the popularity of the subject annoys some people.

Attempts to erase a people and their culture under the guise of serious academic study are delinquent and to be treated with great suspicion. The whole question of Celtic spirituality and religious understanding has been treated in much the same way - a vibrant and evolving approach to the spiritual and mystical, pinned to the table of academic vivisection and slowly cut to pieces until it is unrecognizable. It is no wonder that some academics have trouble finding it, let alone understanding it.

Yes, it is important that we know and understand the facts if we are to make arguments and base ideas upon them. But when it comes to spiritual and religious belief and practice, we are dealing with something that has a dimension that goes well beyond the rational and analytical world of the academic. If we simply play the academic game and reduce the world to nothing but material and analysable facts, we become one with those who are destroying the very world on which we live.

Before we get that far, we enter an unedifying domain where dogmatism reigns - on both sides. Each side misrepresents the other in order to prove petty points and we become bogged down in sterile debates about things that are not important - except perhaps to those who have careers to build and niches to carve.

Facts are important, but the Truth is supreme. Unfortunately, there are those who believe the two to be synonymous. But that cannot be so. The Truth can be related without resorting to the use of facts - that is what a Mystery religion is. The Druids of old spent many years learning to be poets and bards. The whole of their training was based on this understanding and use of language. Nor was it just to convey the facts of this or that genealogy, or of the law. It was also used to formulate the Truth, to teach, to speak of the Mysteries, to enchant, and to immortalize. We might study this, but we cannot reduce it to an exercise in literary criticism any more than we can condemn any interpretation of this system that is itself poetic. If we do, we miss the whole point. Not only of the Druid Way as it was, but of the Way it has since become.

Of one thing we can be certain, the Druid Way was and is part of what is known as the Western Mystery Tradition. It is that part which is derived from the Celtic peoples and their predecessors, from whom they learned a great deal. It is quite distinct from other facets of the Tradition such as Asartu (derived from Nordic peoples) or Odinism (derived from a Saxon/Germanic lineage) in the north, or the Latin and Greek mysteries in the south.

The Western Mystery Tradition is strongly related to the mysteries of the near and middle East. It also has a great deal in common with mystery traditions elsewhere in the world. Whether that is indicative of common Neolithic roots, as some have suggested, is open to debate. But the argument is increasingly convincing the more we learn about the sophistication and mobility of our early ancestors.

Each of these Ways has derived from and reflects a specific geographical location. This occurs through the intermediary of the peoples who live there and who have been shaped by their social and physical environments. Others have not dictated their apprehension and understanding of the divine to them any more than it comes from the abstractions of a book. It has come directly from the world around them, a world with which they were intimately related. Equally, their expression of the divine relates to that world. A Celtic vision of the world informs what we now call the Druid Way.

This is not the Way of robes and paraphernalia and stone circles - slightly skewed outward manifestations beyond which many do not progress. Not the Way of academia which is a sad and dismembered specimen floating palely in its jar until someone else needs it to boost their career. Not the Way of millennia past when the world was a vastly different place.

What we are concerned with is the Way as it is now - a vibrant body that views the world as it is through a Celtic eye and which works to heal the hurts and restore the balance in a way most appropriate to the needs of the land. It is a Way that is firmly rooted in the past, but which grows ever more strongly toward the future. And, like the tree with which it is intimately connected, it is firmly rooted in the soil of the mundane whilst its head is ever in the clouds.

The great core of the tree is the trunk through which and from which all aspects of the Druid Way derive. The roots may draw in from a wide area, but it is a system proportionate to the size and nature of the tree, a system that feeds the growth of the trunk. And from that trunk grow many branches, rooted in the core, but all reaching sunward to give leaf and provide the vital energy necessary for synthesis. The living tree also supports a vast community of other life that interweaves with, takes nourishment from, and provides for the ever-growing entity.

There is a second question, implicit in this first, that needs a distinct response. Starting from where we are means, in effect, choosing a specific Way - one that is best suited to moving us toward the Light. But, choosing a specific Way also means, as we have seen, following a single Way.

This question of a single Way often gets raised, especially by those imbued by the values of our consumer society. Those values must first be shaken off. A quest for the Light is not something to be cobbled together from the choicest selections to be found on some supermarket shelf - discarded or altered when something new and glittering more brightly catches the eye. Sadly, this is all too often the case and reflects not just the values of consumerism but the equally dangerous assumption that we are supreme beings and may do as we choose. That way lies destruction - of the soul and of the world.

Equally, there has been a reaction against the idea of the single Way in recent times because it is perceived, by the superficial eye, as exclusive or as a doctrine of racial purity. These notions are derived from the horrific corruption of spiritual ideologies that we have witnessed over the centuries. But choosing a single Way, whichever one it may be, has nothing to do with these things.

To claim that the Druid Way must be exclusively Celtic is neither racist nor elitist. It is not racist as the Celts do not constitute a race - they are merely a group of peoples with a common metaphysical, cultural, and linguistic heritage. And even if they were a race, it is their way of looking at the world that is important, not their genetic make up. It is not elitist, because it does not exclude any more than it claims to be either the sole or the best of Ways. It is simply a matter of defining that with which we are dealing. The Druid Way is derived from a Celtic metaphysic. If it starts to exclude parts of that or include other things, it ceases to be the Druid Way.

Let us return to the tree. Like the Way, it is an organic entity, growing, evolving. There are many kinds of tree. But they all share common and defining characteristics. You cannot look at a tree and say, 'I like the tree, but I would rather it had feathers than leaves,' or, 'The bark is a bit rough, I would rather it was fur.' If that is your approach, you have no tree; you have no Druid Way. What you do have is a gross act of violence against a naturally evolved system - violence done to the spirit.

But this is not only a matter of definition. There is a much more important point about the nature of any spiritual quest. You cannot pick and mix simply because a Way is a Way - you learn it, you become it, a step at a time. You build a specific structure on specific foundations. If you miss out some steps because they don't suit you, or if you introduce elements from elsewhere, then you are not truly engaged on the Way.

After all, it is not as though the Way we choose were simply akin to walking a path - something that we can get on and off at will or from which we can take short cuts. There are elements of a path. We are making a journey. But it goes much further than that. To talk of being on or following a path is to keep our self separate from it. That is why the term 'Way' is used. It has within it the idea of a path or route, but it also has a much more comprehensive meaning - not just of the path we take, but of how we conduct ourselves along that path, of what we become as we progress.

Progress in the Way should not, however, be confused with the Way itself. Progress is through learning about the Way and moving onward as a result of each new thing that you learn. What you learn about is already there. You integrate with something that pre-exists you. Paradoxically, being on the Way is not just learning about the Way; it is becoming the Way. You learn to become the path that you walk. You do not just study the tree, you become the tree. One tree in a forest, a great community of spirits, each a viable entity that is part of and enriched by the larger whole.

What is more, the Ways themselves are important, one to another and as a whole. They complement each other, learn from each other. A rope made of a single strand, no matter how thick, has neither the strength nor the flexibility of a rope made of many, distinct, and interwoven strands. And the strength lies not just in that distinctness, but in mutualism. By maintaining distinctive diversity, we increase the richness and strength of the many flowers that are to be found in the garden of the divine, the many notes and parts of the song that is sung.

By keeping to a single Way, we harmonize our energies and channel them in a common direction. This gives us greater integrity, strength, flexibility, and protection as well as minimizing the disturbance within our spiritual evolution. Think of a river in which different streams and currents contend with one another. The surface is rough and the undercurrents are dangerous. They can pull you down and keep you under. Think of a river that splits into many channels and tries to go in different directions. It becomes sluggish and loses its way, eventually stagnating.

Many people do not take their spiritual health seriously, which is a terrible mistake. Not only is this bad in itself, but it can also have serious effects on mental and physical well-being. Those who dabble in things they do not understand, or use what they discover for their own hedonistic ends, disturb things at many levels. In so doing, they will hurt themselves. What is worse, they can and will hurt others.

Of course, there would be no problem with any of this if we were all the same, all at the same stage of spiritual development. But we are not. We all come from different places, have different experiences and understandings of the world. Our destination may be a common one; our starting point is not.

None of this is to claim that the Druid Way is well or fully defined, a settled thing. It derives from the natural world and is subject to both change and evolution. Part of being Druid is to be sensitive to that, to understand what we are and what we are becoming. To do that effectively, we have to see with a Celtic eye. But we also have to look beyond the Druid Way to other Ways and traditions to help us fill the gaps in our knowledge and in our understanding. This can be done because there are undoubted similarities between many of the mystery traditions and nature religions and the Way of the Druid. This is not because of borrowing, but because they are manifestations of a single Truth.

Animals and their mystical and totemic function are just one example of this concordance, although there are many variations of detail. The Mother Goddess and her resurrecting son is another. So it is that we have our legitimate interests in Native American spirit ways, in ancient Chinese philosophy, in Buddhism, Shamanism, Gnosticism, the Eleusinian mysteries, Mithras, and so much more. All these things help to colour the picture. Yet an 'interest in', no matter how deep and satisfying, should not be confused with a 'commitment to', or a 'commitment to becoming'.

Commitment to a specific Way is a form of meditation on a grand scale. It is the gradual calming of the mind and focusing of the spirit over many years. To begin with, the enquiring mind darts hither and yon in search of knowledge. Great knowledge. High knowledge. The more it learns, the more it begins to see patterns. As it recognizes and understands the patterns, the knowledge that has been gathered is assimilated and, having done its job, falls away. The more you know, the less you need to know. And as that knowledge falls away, it reveals a growing strand of wisdom upon which the mind and the spirit centres and finds rest. In that wisdom we may, ultimately, discover the way to enlightenment.

It may seem that some of the foregoing has somewhat laboured a number of points. This is quite deliberate. Any Way can be hazardous for the person who has not properly prepared themselves, who does not accept that others have been there and know whereof they speak. There is no intention here to inflate the hazards or to scare you - simply to point out that there are very real dangers to the spirit if you do not take care of it. The same is just as true for the mind and the body.

As already stated, this book will not be about the content and mechanics of ceremonial and ritual, about lore, about Celtic history, about esoteric knowledge. These things can be found in abundance elsewhere. It is an introduction to the metaphysic - the mindset or world view - to be achieved if one is to become fully Druid. It is a mindset very different from the one we are all used to operating by - the one that is forced upon us and deeply ingrained. We have to break down the old patterns and move away from the assumptions about and emphasis on analytical empiricism and on materialism. In doing so, however, we can, if we are not careful, not properly prepared, make ourselves vulnerable for a while to malign influences.

As for esoteric knowledge, the arcane, it is doubtful whether Truth and the Light are to be found hidden away in complex systems of numerology or bizarre ceremonies and experiments. There is a place for systems that are means to an end - number can help us understand some of the patterns of the world; genuine ceremonial and ritual bond us to the world - but if they are allowed to become the be all and end all, they are reduced to nothing but highly destructive acts of violence against the world and against the spirit. Any 'secrets' they reveal are not worth the price. Not only are they tainted by the method used to obtain them, but they also relate only to the narrow system in which the method is based. Their relevance to the world is minimal and anyone who seeks the Truth and the Light in that direction will simply illuminate some small dark corner of the depths of the cave.

True teachings, true knowledge, tend to contextualize, offering a framework that will accommodate the complexities of real life, rather than a rigid system into which real life will not fit without distortion and amputation. It is in an ever more comprehensive understanding of the framework that the 'secret' of Truth and the way to the Light is to be found.

Of necessity, the framework is derived from and firmly rooted in the real world about us. There is no escaping that. Truth may be too precious to hand to any fool who asks for it, but the fool only asks because they are not wise enough to see the Truth where it is - in the open, before their very eyes. Wisdom is in learning to see the world in a fresh way that brings the Truth into sharp and sometimes frightening focus. It is the way our ancestors saw it, but tempered with a knowledge of what the world has since become and how it has reached that pass.

In order to do that, we will be going to a place where the wind blows free and we can, with care and patience, learn to hear the voice it carries. A place where we can ask questions about the fundamentals of our being. Answering or trying to answer does not necessarily commit us to living by what we discover as a result. Questions are seldom asked for that reason, although we do have to live *with* what we have learned. We ask questions and work to answer them because that is how we learn more about the world. And one of the first things we have to learn is that the process never ends.

Asking questions of the world is not like the closed system of an examination. There is no standard answer. There is no pass mark (although there may be a fail mark to which we have come perilously close). The world is spiritually infinite and although it is materially finite, it is infinitely variable. No question asked of an open and infinite system will ever produce a definitive answer. Usually, asking a question will present you with a number of other questions to be explored.

This is one reason why you can only really try to answer questions. There are others. For example, the questions we ask are personal. This does not mean they are purely subjective. Whilst it is true you cannot divorce such questions that we must ask from personal experience, enough persons are involved with a shared frame of reference for us to consider such questions as being objective. That does not, however, divorce them from the personal perspective.

Each question we ask about the world is also a question about how we are related to the world, about our position within it. This precludes any definitive, once and for all answer. Each of us is constantly evolving as a person. The world about us changes without cease. A question is different each and every time we ask it. The answer, therefore, can never be the same.

In many ways it is a frightening prospect. We are not prepared for such exploration of the world by the schooling we receive. The education system serves only the material domain. It is why so many retreat to the material realm and pretend there is no other. They are scared by the vastness that confronts them beyond the cave, much as they are unable to confront the vastness within themselves in moments of silence and stillness.

There is also the point to be borne in mind that, sometimes, no matter how far we might pursue some questions, there is no consensus to be arrived at, no conclusion to be reached, no answer to be had. Many questions are asked because they enable us to get closer to other questions. To expect an outright and definitive answer would be folly.

In the end, we may not be able to find answers to our questions because we are looking for the wrong sort of answers. We are, after all, seeking out the living heart of great mysteries. What we will find is that we must gather sufficient knowledge to realize that knowledge is unimportant; that we must undertake the journey to learn that we belong where we began; that the journey *is* the goal; that learning to wait for a teacher *is* the lesson; asking the question *is* the answer. What we learn along the way is that there is nothing to be learned.

We are all on a journey in which the spirit evolves, stage by stage, leap by leap. We are voracious; our appetite for knowledge is immense. But understanding, wisdom, and if we are lucky, enlightenment, often come after we have turned our back on our studies and returned home from the journey. We find when we no longer seek. But to stop searching we must have been searching to begin with.

There is much that seems paradoxical here. That is why we must always explore this and other questions as thoroughly as we can. That is why we should be wary of making up our minds and never changing them. That is why we should, sometimes, reach a conclusion and hold to it fiercely. That is why we should always, at some stage, forget the journey, forget the search, empty our minds of it all, and sit in the sun with our backs to a tree.

To understand any question, to find any approximation of an answer, the question must be asked. In asking, you have already moved closer to an answer - the one shapes the other. Yet, as we have already observed, when you ask a question often all you get are more questions which spawn their own answer-questions. It can be frustrating and it is often why folk give up on such things for they are too wedded to linear processes. They feel they are going round in circles when they want direction. Yet direction you have, albeit circuitous, for you do not go in circles. Rather, you work the rounds of a spiral. And the spiral slowly tightens and you eventually reach the point of it all.

Understanding is, of course, a noble sentiment. But of what use is it? After all, we each of us have to live in the real world and deal with day-to-day living at the same time as we work to change the world. This may, to some, seem to beg the question. Change the world? Is that what this is all about? How have we moved from spiritual quest to political reform? The short answer is that we have not. The Druid Way is informed by a Celtic sensibility and in that, person, community, and planet are facets of an indissoluble triunity. Change one, and you inevitably change the other two.

It is, however, more complex than simple linear cause and effect. One needs to be able to view the world differently and act differently in accordance with that view - stepping beyond the false boundaries we have been taught to accept. And, of course, you must always start from where you are. With you. For you cannot hope to effect lasting change in the world if you cannot first change yourself. Any more than you can hope to change the world without first identifying what it is that requires change, what you think it should be changed to, and what paths will take you from here to there.

Even that, in the end, is insufficient. It is a good start and will take you a long way, but life is infinitely variable. Whatever plans you may make and whatever pathways you may map out, they will always fall short of expectations or prove to be inappropriate. It seems a hopeless task. This does not mean, however, that we should give up. It simply means that we should prepare ourselves in a way that can cope with the vagaries of the real world.

The best way to do that is to have a sound understanding of the metaphysical stance that will underpin your quest. If you have chosen a Way, it is often done at an emotional or intuitive level. There is nothing wrong in this, our instincts are often more trustworthy than our intellect - especially as our intellectual structures are based on flawed materialistic notions. But that does not mean that once you have chosen, you should not then come to know and understand the basis of that for which you have opted. Indeed, it would be extremely difficult to avoid and irresponsible not to do so.

In a sense, this is about learning theories in order to better one's practise. Of course, that is an extremely crude way of expressing it. Even if we could in some useful way say what theories we are talking about, there is far more to the situation than simply learning them and then applying them to a given situation. Human beings do not work in that way. Spiritual development does not lend itself to such simplistic procedures.

The word 'theory' has a wide range of meaning and there are many kinds of theory operating at many different levels. These range from rules-of-thumb which are derived from everyday experience, through more complex empirical generalizations, to the most abstruse of notions concerning the universe. At the rule-of-thumb end of the scale, the application of theory is simple. Such theories are rarely complex and have a very narrow range of application. They are almost always derived from specific experiences within given situations and the link between theory and practice, although simple, is quite intimate.

The more complex and generalized a theory becomes, however, the wider is its application. With that, its link with everyday happenings and experience seems to become more tenuous. When we come to consider the seeming complexities of metaphysical thinking, it is little wonder that many people see in it no relevance of any kind to their everyday lives.

It is not just the apparent complexity of metaphysical exploration that causes problems. The whole practice of philosophy has been hugely discredited by the rise of the professional academic philosophers - people paid to think and, in most cases, dissect what others have thought and taught about it. This is so divorced from real concerns, so sterile an activity, that it has blighted itself almost out of existence. Those involved certainly have no love of wisdom.

One of the major problems of academic philosophy is that it has shied away from the fundamental questions that face us. Indeed, it has tried to become a branch of linguistics, reducing everything to a question of the use of language. Granted, it is always important to be clear about what you mean when you use language, as it is open to a great deal of ambiguity and misuse. But that does not mean that wider and more abstruse questions cannot be debated because they have been deemed 'meaningless'. Common sense tells us they are not.

Philosophy is not an activity divorced from the world any more than it is an end in itself. Philosophy is a love of and search for wisdom. Yet wisdom, as we have already observed, is not something to be shut away in a book or a classroom. It cannot be frozen or ossified. Wisdom is a living thing, a light that illuminates our path through the world, a light that allows us to see the patterns. This gives meaning to our lives. Meaning does not and never has resided in the questions of philosophers. In that, they have missed the point. Meaning is in those for whom the questions are important. Wisdom is a potential within us to understand the world. The questions are simply one, albeit important, way of releasing that potential.

Unfortunately, and despite our common sense (or intuitive faculty), we are all too willing to listen to the nagging empirical inner voice to which we are all heir. As a result we shy away from metaphysical problems because we are led to believe that they have no relevance in this day and age. Unfortunately, this is not true. In fact, we need to address these problems now more than ever. We need to understand the metaphysical basis of our being and we need to know and understand how this can be used to improve ourselves, our communities, and the planet.

It is fairly easy to demonstrate how someone such as a builder, for example, can relate their theoretical knowledge to their work as a builder. They know about the generalized properties of materials, quantities required, the standards that exist for certain work, even the formulae for calculating stress and the forces involved in a given construction. This knowledge of general principles and regulations, along with past experience, is used by the builder in the design and construction of specific types of building.

This can be taken a step further to consider how, for example, a doctor uses their theoretical knowledge and experience in specific applications. We have moved on by many magnitudes of complexity from the builder and their inanimate structures. The doctor, after all, is dealing with a far more complex and variable system than any builder will ever face. At this level of complexity, the doctor is involved not only in applying theoretical knowledge of anatomy, physiology, disease, and the like to the human body, but they are also engaged in making judgements over and above what is wrong with a person and how to treat them. Many other factors come into play, not least because human beings are involved and there is a relationship between the two to be considered as well as any social and psychological effects.

For all the complexities involved in medicine, we can still say that the field is finite. We can also easily see the link between theoretical knowledge and practice. Once we move beyond the finite, we move into a different realm. Here, the subject matter is tenuous and infinite in scope. Knowing it and understanding it is difficult enough. Relating it to the practice of everyday life would seem, at first glance, to be impossibly complex.

In the preceding, and in all similar cases, a judgement of value is implied in the application of theory to practice. The builder assumes (usually without considering the point) that it is good or right to apply their theoretical knowledge and their experience to their practical work. The same is true for doctors. It is a good thing to heal people. Indeed, it is often the value judgement that provides the impetus to learn the theory and then apply it.

Also implied is the fact that theories do not exist in isolation. They are evolved by people and they are held by people. Without people, theories would not exist and they could not be applied. This is a point that is all too often forgotten or lost to view. For all that, there is a sense in which rules-of-thumb, building theory, anatomy, or any other such sets of theoretical knowledge can be regarded as distinct (though never separate) from the person or persons who know and understand them. When we get to the level of metaphysics this changes.

At this level, the term 'application' becomes inadequate to describe the relationship between theory and practice. Even the aspect of value judgements moves into a new area of complexity. Whilst those engaged in metaphysical exploration are convinced of the worth of careful judgements of value, they are also acutely aware of the fact that discussion and understanding of the very basis of what is good and right are themselves part of the realm of metaphysics.

Before we get tied into knots over that, however, we should return to the main theme of this argument. Whereas coming to know and understand areas of theoretical knowledge may be difficult and their practical application strenuous and complex, there is a sense (already mentioned) in which such theoretical knowledge is distinct from the person who applies it and derives experience from that application. With metaphysics, that distinction vanishes.

The key word here is 'distinction'. No one can undergo even the simplest experience without it changing them. Learning is far from simple. This means that each person is engaged in much more than a mere relationship with what they learn. What you learn actually changes you. At a simple level the change is not great, although even then it can be profound. Generally speaking, however, the change will have an effect only in areas relating to the specific field of the theory and its related practice. A person's outlook, their mental model of the world, is largely the same.

Increasing one's store of knowledge simply enables a person to undertake an increased range of tasks. It is like getting a new tool to add to a tool kit. With the new tool, the range of tasks available to a person is increased. But the nature of the tool kit is much the same and there is no radical shift in the sort of work that can be done any more than there is likely to be a shift in the attitude of a person to their life in general as a result. Even a doctor, who must encompass huge and complex fields of knowledge, is able to distinguish between that and their general view of the world. If not, then all doctors would think the same about all things - which they manifestly do not.

With metaphysics, we cease to tinker with aspects of our understanding that are on the surface of our being. With metaphysics we stop adding tools to our tool kit. With metaphysics we begin to dismantle and reconstruct our understanding of everything, even the nature of understanding itself. All tools go out. Their very nature is examined along with the nature of the work they enable us to do. It is a task that requires a huge leap of faith because everything we have ever taken for granted comes under scrutiny.

This part of our quest takes us into the very heart of the unknown, which lies within us. Many mystery religions and spiritual Ways re-enact this during the initiation of adherents. Left alone in the darkness of a cave or purpose built structure, initiates would experience the pre-natal darkness that comes before re-birth as a reconstructed person - one who has stripped away all the old assumptions and started on the Way to Truth.

The journey into darkness is balanced by the journey back to the light. Most cultures depict this with a journey to the heart of a labyrinth or spiral. Some see a darkness in the centre where one must confront a monster and destroy it. The symbolism is obvious. In order to reach the Light, one must destroy the darkness within one's self. Within Celtic lore, there is a subtle difference in understanding - a recognition that Light and Dark are inseparable parts of a single cycle and that one must know one in order to know the other, that balance is all important.

All too often, this is mistaken for the linear dualism popularized by Descartes, just as it is often used as an excuse for evil - for without evil, the argument runs, we cannot have good. Linear dualism is based on specious assertions, and systems built upon the notion have no credibility. They are however a timely reminder that when we work at this level, it is absolutely essential that we are thorough in our thought and wholehearted in our practice.

Recognising the inextricable link between theory and practice is essential. Many do not. They read about the Celtic past, they dress up, they play. They are just one of those groups in the playground. They have knowledge about things, but to have a thing is to create a distinction between it and the self. It is not enough simply to know about a thing, it must also inform all actions as well. To take to the Druid Way is a becoming. To be something is to admit unity with it. That is why we talk about *being* Druid. It is something we evolve towards, it is a metaphysical stance, it is what we are.

Of course, becoming Druid is not something that happens one day and that is an end of it. It is a constant evolution, a constant refinement, a constant search. This makes it sound as though it were a special and constant effort being Druid. In a sense that is true. One of the important aspects of ritual and ceremonial is that it helps to reinforce that commitment. But that is only part of the story, for although ritual and ceremony may reinforce the commitment to the Druid Way, it does not create the underlying metaphysic. This comes from a shift in perspective, based on Celtic sensibilities, but derived from a personal encounter with the world when one has stripped away the preconceptions that have been dinned into us.

The Druid Way is a very personal commitment. There is no creed, there are no rules set out in a code for anyone to see - universally accepted and readily applied. The Druid Way is not derived from a fixed teaching, but from mutable nature. We each make ourselves in the world's image, appropriate to our task.

To an outsider, to one who does not understand, the Druid Way seems to be an anarchic, make-it-up-as-you-go-along sort of a thing. Nothing could be further from the truth. Mutability and evolution are facts of our existence. The Druid Way recognizes this and instead of trying to erect a rigid structure that would be irrelevant before it was finished, it has, over the centuries, grown with the times, true to its core but adapting to new climates. It is why it still exists.

As such, each Druid constantly assesses what they are and what they are becoming. Their values are enshrined in the reality of existence, rooted deeply in the soil, flexible enough to bend before any wind. And because such values reach into the real world beyond the confines of a fixed system learned by rote, they are fundamental and interpenetrating. Each Druid has to think these thoughts through, live in them and for them, become them.

The great danger in any Way is that tags and catchwords from what once may have been a living wisdom are reduced to catch-all formulae for all to follow (and to fail miserably in following). It is quite useless to learn the 'correct' codes of conduct - even if there were such a thing. It is not in this that the essence of the Druid Way is to be found. Nor does it have to do with anything so simplistic as putting theory into practice. That is where the journey begins, but if it is to become a true spiritual quest it must go beyond the whole notion of making the thoughts, values and commitment's of the Way one's own.

Metaphysical thinking is about coming to understand why there is a universe and why we are a part of it. It is to do with our relationship with everything else. That means we must know who we are, we must forge ourself from ourself for ourself. But we cannot do that in isolation. We are each a distinct but integral part of the universe and we are shaped by it, especially those parts with which we have the greatest and most intimate contact. But striving to get beyond that in order to understand the fundamental questions (let alone find any answers) is far more than an intellectual exercise with practical offshoots. There is a motivating force behind the intellectual search and the practice of what we learn. That force is emotion.

Emotion is evoked by our personal involvement with the universe. We may use our intellect to help us, but the dynamic behind it all is desire. A desire to understand, a desire to be at peace, a desire to be as one, a belief that satisfying these desires is a good thing for ourselves and for the world. To achieve this we use our intellectual and intuitive faculties to equip us with ideas and understanding which then become integral to our personal being. These are not things that are tacked on - available in some separate compartment for use only when needed. They are genuinely integrated.

This level of exploration and the integration into our being of what we discover occurs as a result of our personal involvement in their discovery and re-creation. Whereas we might accept what we are told by someone else about the nature of the universe and our place in it, it has little real effect on us. We accept it intellectually, but it does not touch us. If we then explore such an idea for ourselves, even if we come to the same conclusion, we have become personally involved. And once we involve our very person, we cannot help but change at a fundamental level of our being.

When it comes to this degree of involvement with the universe, if it is not you, it is nothing. When a thing becomes part of you, it alters your whole being. Nothing is ever just tacked on. A thing absorbed transforms the whole structure of the self so that a new whole constantly comes into being. Once you have reached this level, you become open to and part of all that you interact with. Every meal you eat, every conversation you have, every dream you dream, every book you read, every hand you hold, every hole you dig, every plant you nurture, every star you watch... They reshape you. You reshape them. If a thing has not changed, been absorbed by you, become part of you and your being, it is nothing. It simply does not exist.

Eventually the universe becomes absorbed into the person and the person absorbed into the universe. You are bound to the rest of creation in a way that is open to all, but rarely accepted. All your dispositions become subtly changed and your outlook altered. You see the world differently, you know the world differently, you act differently. And as the false barrier between thought and action has also been breached, you act more instinctively in line with the way of the universe.

If you have come this far, your first steps on your quest will have taken you a long way. They are frightening steps to take. It is a wonderful journey to make. A journey into the future. Yet for all that we have our head in the clouds, we must keep our feet firmly on the ground. For all that we are concerned with the future, we must never neglect the past.

Coming to know the past is a restoration of the past, a replanting of the forests of the soul that have been destroyed. We cannot recreate what was. The seasons have turned too many times. But we can look to what sustained us in the past and seek ways of ensuring that replenishment in the future - adapting to circumstances as need requires. Without that, we will lose the forest altogether.

For this task we need wisdom. Some talk of an Ancient Wisdom, but the wisdom we require is ever present and much more difficult to come to terms with than any escapist secret doctrine composed of mumbo-jumbo. The wisdom is in us and all around us. It is there to be read in the book of the world, but first we must learn how to read. For that, we must slow down, cast off the inessential, work simply, and touch the earth. We must also learn to sit quietly and observe with open eyes, open heart, open spirit, open mind. It means not only that we must look, but also that we must see.

In the end, it comes down to everyday life and the simple things we must do to sustain our being without impact upon the earth. That is where the secrets are to be found - not in thinking that, but in doing that. That is the mark of how easy and of how difficult it will be. The simple basics of life are now so often held in contempt. Yet if we cannot and do not embrace them with love, if we are unable to get them right, ours is a hopeless case.

That, then, is where we are.

That is always from where we must start.

IS THE DRUID WAY A RELIGION?

Is the Druid Way a religion? This is a question fundamental to understanding the Druid Way. It is one that needs to be confronted (sooner rather than later) by all who follow the Way and by all who are contemplating whether or not to do so. It is not, as one can imagine, an easy question to resolve.

Unfortunately, the people you might first think of going to for guidance cannot agree. There are some Druids who assert that the Druid Way *is* a religion and there are others who assert that it is *not* a religion. This would, on the face of it, seem to be a classic dilemma - an either/or situation that inevitably leads to some form of conflict. This is not least because those who have come to some decision and made their assertions are Druids - people for whom Truth is paramount, people who have a propensity to examine things carefully before making pronouncements on them. They will, it is to be hoped, have invested a great deal of time and effort in such considerations. And one of those groups must be right. And one of those groups must be wrong. Mustn't they?

The question also needs to be confronted because of the public conception of Druids and the Druid Way. This, quite naturally, is formulated from the public face of the Druid Way, which is seldom seen and somewhat allusive.

One of the many functions of a Druid is to know and preside over the eight ceremonies that mark the inner and outer stations of the year. In form, these ceremonies resemble what most people would regard as religious activity. As some of these ceremonies are conducted in public, the question of religion is one that is most commonly assumed about and asked of Druids by those who stand outwith the Grove.

This matter is complicated by the fact that many of the public ceremonies ascribed to Druids are often conducted in outlandish costume and at controversial places. The picture presented to non-Druids is therefore false, biased by the activities of those who are still in the playground.

To complicate matters further, there are factions within the 'established' religions (mostly Christianity) which all too often have a vested interest in their own supremacy. These tend to be the groups that are most critical of pagans and pagan activity. They have influence beyond their importance and display an appalling degree of ignorance about what pagan is and pagan does. They deny that the Druid Way (or any other pagan belief) can be a religion, much as they deny that any creed or sect but their own can be a religion. However, they often go much further and falsely equate the likes of the Druid Way with the unsavoury practices of the personified evil of their own theology. Such denigration has been going on for many centuries and, if for no other reason, it is important that the wilful ignorance that fuels such accusations is countered with the Truth.

That such discussion and exploration of the question has been going on for so long without resolution may be thought strange. But the reason for that is fairly straightforward. At one time, even to discuss the idea openly would have put a person at risk of accusations of heresy and being burned at the stake. The gradual change in climate that allowed discussion was occasioned by the rise of so-called rational thought. Discussion was acceptable, the subject was sidelined. However, because a subject is neither wholly or partly within the realms of the rational does not mean it should be dismissed - otherwise we would have to dismiss the reality and impact of love, music, art, and all other non-rational aspects of our life and being.

On a personal level there are also many reasons why we avoid discussing or, if we discuss, reaching conclusions on such issues. Two, in particular, are common to us all. The first is that we are often (and validly so) wary of committing ourselves outright to a particular position. What if we are wrong? Failure, after all, is something we have been taught to despise. The other reason (which is really the same reason stated positively), is that we tend to believe it is far better to be well informed and develop a wisdom that will allow us to react to and work in the real world rather than pervert things to conform to a specific creed. Unfortunately, this frequently results in a frustrating attitude of non-committal that is often seen as one of the characteristics of so-called New Age thinking. Commitment is not necessarily a bad thing. It is possible to hold on to something tightly as long as we are equally prepared to let go lightly.

There is also a curious phenomenon associated with many such difficult topics. That is that we think we know what the answer is. And believing that, we never go any further. It is not until we actually have to put it into words that we realize how inadequate is our understanding. Once you try to articulate what you think you know, you find that the concept is far more difficult to unravel and tie down than you had imagined. Words seem to be inadequate for the task. And this is partly the case. We are, after all, talking of mystical things.

Words are not *wholly* inadequate, as many mystics have demonstrated. Indeed, a careful choice of words can readily express the many layered meaning of challenging concepts and open our minds to what lies beyond. They are but symbols and that is their function. It is just that we lack practice in their use.

Also important to remember is that in asking a question, we have a responsibility to consider what effect a given answer may have. This does not mean we are bound by the answer. Not all answers are of that kind. But the Truth, should we be fortunate enough to find it, is a heavy burden to bear. After all, if we conclude that the Druid Way is not a religion, what then is it? What function does it serve or, more appositely, *who* does it serve? And where does that leave (in our world if that of no one else) those who do believe it to be religion? Conversely, if we conclude that it is a religion, what of those who do not accept this? How do we accommodate their presence in the Grove? We should not, of course, allow worry over the answers to prevent us from exploring the question. It is just that we must be aware of and take responsibility for the consequences of what we do.

Before we can begin to answer the original question, however, we need to ask two others. The first of these is, 'What is religion?' and the second is, 'What is the Druid Way?' Nothing if not abstruse.

What is religion?

In discussing religion, it is important to be clear that we are *not* discussing religions. That is, we are considering an abstract rather than actual and particular systems of religious belief. This is not a clear-cut distinction because the notion of religion is inextricably bound up with actual religions. Indeed, there is a very real sense in which religion *per se* does not exist. There is not a perfect religion; there is not a concept, an abstract, or an idea that pre-existed actual religions of which individual religions are but examples or realizations. Religions came first, born of our desire to understand the mysteries of being. Religion came later, born of a desire to understand the desire to understand the mysteries of being.

To say that a religion exists to satisfy our desire to understand the mysteries of being does not fully convey its role in our lives. A religion does not exist in order simply to explain the world - that is done partly by science. A religion exists to provide a means of integrating the world, bringing together the whole realm of experience and understanding in a unified whole.

This is not to say that any religion has succeeded, notwithstanding what many adherents have claimed through the millennia. Religion may provide the means of integration, but it also reveals that there is a great deal of mystery in the world, and it is right that there should be. We need mystery in our lives. It provides the dynamic that moves us to explore. It also constantly reminds us that there are things far greater than us, things that we cannot understand, things that we cannot control.

Without that, we lose all sense of proportion - we become arrogant and we become dangerous.

This element of mystery (and there are others) is sufficient to explain why any discussion of religion is fraught with difficulty. It is not simply a matter of discussing a set of propositions. Religion encompasses much that goes beyond normal experience and understanding. This is not because it is difficult or open only to a chosen few. It is simply that our approach to the world, the way in which we are taught to look at things, is biased against anything that is not material or analysable, against anything that cannot be bought, possessed, and consumed. Religion is none of those things. Rather, it is an absolute and unifying experience of the world that transfigures human existence from that of self-centred destructiveness to creative immanence.

Such transfiguration exists in potential within us all. It cannot be encompassed within the rational world, as the rational is a partial form of understanding. Religion, however, can and does encompass the rational. It is, after all, a mark of religious experience that we become enlightened to greater or lesser degree. Enlightenment is a form of gnosis - a knowing - and knowledge of the world needs to be assimilated into our understanding. This is a form of rationalization, especially when it involves discussion with other people. Enlightenment is rarely complete and instantaneous. For most of us it is a gradual process achieved through study, meditation, and work in the world.

Rationalization plays its part in the social cohesion of a religion as well as in its evolution. Religion is, after all, a shared experience of the world, one that is transmitted from generation to generation. The world changes. People change. If a religion cannot have its central beliefs clearly expressed, then they cannot be conveyed from person to person. Without that, those beliefs have no chance of reaching fruition as the fully developed metaphysical notions that guide our actions in the world.

Within Contemporary Western Society, however, there has been an increasing trend toward the analysis of religion - a trend that has developed out of the strange schism that exists between religious and secular life. Those who are truly religious understand religion. But it is secular society that is predominant and which constantly tries to understand religious belief and its persistence in the face of what secular society claims is overwhelming evidence of the purely material.

Proponents of secular society and of materialistic thought are engaged in a constant search for certainty. When it comes to religion, they demand incontrovertible proof of the claims made by religion. But that is to misunderstand what religion is (a misunderstanding also not uncommon amongst those who claim to be religious). The error is inherent in using the wrong tools for the job (science) or misusing the correct tools (philosophy).

Certain aspects of religion are open to empirical investigation. One can study its history, its social impact, its artefacts. But they are peripherals, distinct forms of expression of what lies at the mysterious heart. That is well beyond the rational, beyond proof, beyond empirical certainty.

Religion is also extremely personal. No matter that it may have a commonly agreed core and derive from outwith the person, we each react to it in ways appropriate to our own understanding and level of development. This is not open to empirical assessment for all that some bluster it must be so. There comes a point in our personal search where it is necessary to leave behind the safe and familiar world. It is this leap of faith that takes us beyond what is open to rational examination. It is in this leap of faith that we part company with those whose timidity leaves them with the toys that they are dismantling in the playground.

At this point, those wedded to rationalism begin to get a little irrational themselves. Those that do not stoop to insult, usually spend an inordinate amount of time trying to sideline religion. Why they should be so obsessed with doing so is, itself, something of a mystery. After all, it is not unreasonable to go beyond reason and allow our emotions and intuitive faculties to play a central and creative role in exploring and learning about the vast unknown that surrounds us. We have these gifts, so why not use them?

Religion cannot be bounded by empirical thought or a material approach. Nor can it be considered an intellectual exercise. This is simply because religion is deeply rooted in emotional experience. The closest that rationalism can come is in discussing the experiences that we have had. Rationalism works as a descriptive exercise. It can never be successfully prescriptive.

Even then, the descriptive exercise is fraught with problems. What is being discussed is a flash of insight, a moment of gnosis, an understanding so comprehensive that it is overwhelming. The desire to share is enormous because the religious experience is invariably of unity. But we are back to one of the problems we started with. Understanding and describing that understanding are two distinct things. When the understanding is so wholly inclusive, it is difficult to know where to begin. And while there is a feeling that it must be shared, there is also a very strong sense that to analyse it is to lose the very essence of the experience.

A religious experience is one that has a profound effect on a person, not just transforming their whole understanding of the universe, but also completing that understanding. After such an experience a person realizes who they are, what life is all about, their place in the scheme of things, the unity of all being. Exactly how the experience (or set of experiences) is interpreted depends on the culture, ideas, and language of the person involved.

Such an experience breaks down all the barriers that we have been taught to build between ourselves and the external world. It takes us beyond ourselves and makes evident the underlying unity of all things. The normal limitations of time and space, along with the physical senses, are dissolved to the point where there is no longer any definable difference between the self and the rest of creation. The distinction between subject and object is broken down. Be that as it may, although the barriers dissolve and there is an overwhelming sense of unity with all things, the self is never lost. Religion, therefore, is as much about the self as it is about the divine, as much about the relationship between the two as it is about either.

With this change of perspective comes a sense of joy and of having returned home. There, one becomes aware of the ultimate Truth - a knowledge so profound and absolute it simply cannot be put into words. This means that the experience itself cannot become a religion. It is far too personal and certainly not open to being conventionalized and organized.

It is the changed person and their need to live in accordance with their vision that gives rise to religion. It becomes a means by which the experience can be transmitted to others, no matter how imperfectly, and by which others can be brought toward an understanding of the experience, if not the experience itself. The differences between particular religions derive from the cultural interpretation of the experience.

The formalized expression of the religious experience is what becomes what we know of as religion. Whereas the experience is intensely personal, religion is social. It takes that ineffable vision as a model of existence, setting up formal structures within which people can live in such a way that their every action is an expression of that vision. At the same time, the structures provide the means by which people can be brought, under guidance, to a state in which they are open to such experience as well.

Religion is, therefore, 'an organism of many dimensions typically encompassing doctrines, myths, ethical teachings, rituals, and social institutions, all of which are animated by religious experiences of various kinds'. This definition, adapted from that given by Ninian Smart in his book, *The Religious Experience of Mankind*, helps us along our way, but it does have obvious problems in that one of the things used to define religion is religious experience. Religious experience only has meaning as a concept when we know what religion is. There needs to be something more.

For the moment, however, we will consider the definition that has been offered. Smart suggests that there are six essential dimensions to the organism. These are the ritual (pragmatic and sacred), mythological, doctrinal, ethical, social, and experiential dimensions. To these might be added three others: the charismatic, the historical/traditional, and the artistic. These last three are important elements in specific religions, but are not essential to religion itself.

Ritual is one of the ways in which religion tends to express itself. Established forms of worship, prayer, ceremonial, festivals, offerings, and the like are features common to all religions. Ritual need not be elaborate any more than it needs to be derived directly from doctrine. Yet whatever its nature and origin, its purpose is quite clear. Through solemn and customary acts or systems, the intention is to create a space and a moment that transcends time and place in which there can be a communion with the divine. This is sacred ritual.

There is another, distinct form of ritual - pragmatic ritual - that has roughly the same ends as sacred ritual, but which belongs in those religions that do not aspire to direct communion with the divine. The techniques of training and self-discipline involved are analogous to sacred ritual. However, rather than creating a transcendent place for communion, pragmatic ritual is directed toward attaining states of consciousness that will move the practitioner from worldly experience to mystical experience. The intention is to bring the practitioner closer to their goal of nirvana.

Pragmatic ritual may be distinct from sacred ritual, but they do have much in common. This is particularly so in that they both require outer and inner working as well as being aimed toward creating a place in space and time that is outside both. Nor are sacred and pragmatic ritual mutually exclusive. There are, after all, well established traditions of mysticism within religions that aspire to communion with the divine as well as religions that aspire to different and appropriate levels of the divine.

Whatever its content, ritual is exceedingly important to religious expression. In a field of experience where there is a distinct lack of certainty, it provides a degree of stability. Furthermore the repetition involved, provided it does not become mere habit, forms a bond between person and belief that is constantly reinforced. Of course, physical or outer ritual is insufficient on its own to create this. Outer ritual on its own is so much humbug. It must be accompanied by and be in harmony with an inner spiritual intention or ritual. The obverse, however, is a different matter for inner ritual *is* sufficient for an enlightened soul to create the necessary space, as theirs is the return path on the spiral. This in no way diminishes the importance of an harmonic outer ritual as this not only forms a personal bond, but also a social bond that binds together, through common experience, all those within a belief community.

In addition to ritual, every religion has a corpus of myth. Sometimes these myths form a coherent narrative and relate to the core of the religion. Indeed, they sometimes represent the only oral or written tradition that is available. In other religions they are somewhat peripheral to the core beliefs but are, nonetheless, important to an understanding of the religion.

The word 'myth' is often taken to mean a wholly fictional story about the far distant past. In this way, myths are dismissed as irrelevant. Yet they are far too potent a force to be disposed of so easily. A myth is a traditional story that embodies religious ideas or supernatural concepts. Told and retold, they are refined and densely packed vehicles that convey huge amounts of emotional information and connect to us all on a very deep level of our being. The question of the historical veracity of their content is neither relevant nor important.

What *is* important about myths is the Truth that is to be found embedded within them. The stories relate, often in highly symbolic form, many aspects of religious and spiritual teaching and behaviour. Such stories being historically factual would simply be an added bonus in the eyes of some, strengthening their significance. There is a formidable element of belief involved in this, with myth and reality merging - something that can be confusing for outsiders. It would be wrong, however, to assume that adherents of a given religion cannot or will not tell the difference between fact and fiction. It does happen, but not of necessity. In fact, it is a mark of true religion that an adherent *can* tell the difference and is encouraged to do so.

The third dimension is doctrine, which is the attempt to both systematize and clarify what has been revealed by experience. This is done through the medium of ritual and by the use of myth. In creating doctrine, there is a conscious attempt to provide an intellectual dimension to what is revealed. Although the aim is to produce a coherent body of teachings, creating systems and producing clarity do not always go hand in hand. Indeed, systems can inhibit the exploration of the often difficult and seemingly conflicting symbolism and ideas of the religion.

To further confuse matters, the differences between myth and doctrine are often very slight. They are often two ways of approaching the same Truth with myth being intuitive and doctrine being intellectual. This is reflected in the nature of the material involved and of those who approach it. The intuitive soul accepts and even delights in the wildness of the 'raw' mythology in which they can lose themselves, whereas the intellectual soul strives to create an ordered coherence that they can control.

Indeed, a great deal can be revealed about a religion and its adherents from the degree to which doctrine is considered important. Many scholars, for what their opinion is worth, consider religions at the intuitive end of the scale to be 'primitive'. Rigidity and intellectualism are obviously considered to be signs of sophistication, maturity, even progress. It is, perhaps, an attempt to paint religion with the limited colours available to analytical thought. Whatever the case may be, the greater the importance of doctrine within a religion, the more we find that reliance is placed on the need to conform unquestioningly to and stay within a system that was originally intended to make exploration easier.

Adherence to doctrine is one of the many elements of the behaviour of an individual with which religion concerns itself. Behaviour is an important outward sign of the degree to which an individual has been shaped by their religious experience. It is normal for a religion to incorporate a code of ethics into its teachings. Such a code will usually refer to the religious motivation of conduct and to the practical direction of the lives of people. Some are very simple, broad guidelines encapsulated in a single phrase. Others are minutely detailed sets of rules that leave no aspect of behaviour unregulated.

In addition to the rules, there are often sanctions in place to urge adherents to due observance of the rules. These can be both immediate and long term; this worldly and otherworldly. It is generally the case that the more complex an ethical code, the greater and more complex the number of sanctions. These levels of 'sophistication' also reflect the degree to which adherents are allowed to exercise their freedom of will.

There is, of course, a great deal of difference between the ethical teachings of a religion and the actual behaviour of those who claim to follow that faith. In many cases, a religion will set an ethical standard to which it expects adherents to aspire rather than make perfect attainment. Because of this, some argue that the teachings and the observance of those teachings should be considered separately. In terms of defining religion, this may be valid. When it comes to actual religions, it is a different matter. Religions have and still do play a major - if not absolute - part in moulding the ethics of the societies in which they exist. For this reason, the argument for separation should be treated with caution when applied to an actual religion.

The ethical dimension of religion is indicative of the fact that a religion is not merely a system of belief. It also has a cohesive power to bind people together into a community, living their lives in accordance with that belief. It is also a social organization with structures, functions, networks of relationships, and communal patterns of behaviour that have a social significance both for those who hold to that system and for those who do not.

The social shape of a religion is inevitably formed by its religious and ethical ideas and practices. It is also true that the ethical ideals and practices of a religion are shaped by or adapted to the existing social conditions and attitudes in which the belief system first comes into being. It will also be shaped by the social climate of other peoples if it spreads beyond the society of its origin. How far such ideals can be adapted to new social climes before the religion becomes something else depends, of course, on how essential such ideals are considered to be to the identity of the religion.

This depends largely on the degree to which a specific religion is the product of its time and place of genesis as well as the people in which it finds expression. Some have a more universal appeal than others, although it is always dangerous to assume this is simply because of the religion itself. There are many non-religious factors involved in the spread and 'acceptance' of a religion.

For all that, it must be remembered that the wellspring of all religion is experience. Rather, religious experience is the wellspring. Without such experience there would be no religion, nor any of the dimensions discussed above, for it is that experience from which everything else derives and to which everything relates.

The nature of religious experience is extremely varied and wide ranging - from the prosaic to the sublime. At the prosaic end of the scale, where most of us find ourselves, religious experience is derived from any kind of conscious activity concerned with religious concepts or phenomena - prayer, reading a sacred text, even cleaning a place of worship. This may be humble, but it is not to be despised for it is in the everyday that we make sacrifice. At the other end of the scale are those direct experiences of the transcendent and the divine, of the mysteries that cannot be taught or truly shared except with others who have also experienced them. It is in the hope of this last that many come to religion and stay faithful to it. It is in hope of this last that many continue their daily acts of prosaic experience.

Any discussion of or attempt to describe religious experience presents us with special difficulties. The very nature of such an experience puts it largely beyond words, wholly beyond analysis. This is not to say that many haven't tried and, to some extent, succeeded. Ultimately, however, the only way to understand fully such communion with the divine is to experience it for one's self.

The context of such an experience must always be kept in mind when considering the content and form of any description. Much of the language and symbolism used will be specific to the person giving the account and will be highly coloured by their prior social status and religious beliefs as well as their own attitude to such things. Experience - or rather, relating the experience - and doctrine often influence each other quite strongly.

Nor does this mean that those who equate divinity with the world about them, or who believe the divine is simply beyond us at this stage, are incapable of such sublime experience. It is, indeed, the very transcendence of the universe that is most commonly cited as the 'primitive' spur to the religious impulse. This is a clear example of how belief and an understanding of the world influences the nature of the experience and the way in which it is interpreted.

Within those religions that are based on revelation through a chosen mouthpiece, there is some argument that the idea of religious experience of the divine is contrary to that revelation. The central plank of this argument is that divine wisdom and law can only be revealed through an individual chosen mouthpiece and transmitted by their 'legitimate' representatives. This ignores the fact that the revealed wisdom and law has come through the religious experience of an individual who then recounts it to others through an oral tradition or through writings. And through these accounts others will achieve some degree of religious experience without ever challenging the notion of inerrancy held by religions based on revelation.

Most people will content themselves with gaining some sense of the divine through ritual. They will, doubtless, also maintain a hope of some direct communion with the divine. Such experience, of course, means a great deal more than mere awareness. This is where the great step is made - the step from faith to knowledge, the step from belief to certainty.

Knowledge and certainty, experience of the mystery, these are not necessary for religiousness in the many. Faith is sufficient - and in many ways it is the more difficult for the person to live with as it comes always with doubt. Faith requires a sustained effort on the part of the faithful, not least because faith can be twisted and the faithful can be misled.

Knowledge is not an easy burden to bear, either, but the changes that come with it provide a certainty and an energy that sustains the one that knows. It also removes one from the dangers of manipulation. From the ranks of the faithful are recruited the armies that kidnap and slaughter, which ravage the planet with their zeal. From the ranks of the knowing, no one is recruited to the cause of another. They serve only the Light.

The six dimensions discussed above can be brought together into two distinct groups. The first is 'belief', which is comprised of the doctrinal, mythological, and ethical dimensions. The second is 'practice' which is comprised of the ritual, social, and experiential dimensions. The distinction between these two groups - as with the dimensions themselves - is far from hard and fast. After all, if you are genuinely religious, you practice what you believe and you believe what you practice.

Beyond this core, which is essential to all religions, there are a number of other distinct dimensions that are important to specific religions. Foremost amongst these is the charismatic dimension. A number of religions are based upon the revelation vouchsafed to and through a particular individual. But revelation to an individual is insufficient in itself to warrant a distinct dimension. Many people have messages revealed to them from an apparently divine source. Very few have the personality to persuade others that their message is genuinely divinely inspired. Fewer still have the power to convince large numbers of people of this. Less than a handful have had their message passed down from generation to generation.

This, of course, applies to those religions that are derived from the life and works of an individual and refers to the attraction, inspiration, authority, and example of that person. But it goes further. Any religion based on or around an individual will inspire individuality in others as well as encouraging cults of personality. And where the religion outlasts the lifetime of the individual that inspired it, there will inevitably be prominent adherents, saints and mystics, martyrs and teachers, who also exert a charismatic influence.

Although not essential to religious definition, all religions have an historical dimension. Whereas the mythological dimension is concerned with the symbolic importance of past events - real or imagined - the historical dimension of religion is concerned with the path of a religion through time and how it has influenced and been influenced by social forces distinct from itself.

There is a close connection here with the social dimension. Religions tend to be universalist (in theory at least, but with many notable exceptions). They are supposed to look beyond the boundaries of tribe, nation, race, gender, class, or society to offer a message of general significance for humanity. In such cases, it is the awareness of belonging to a living movement with sacred origins in the past, as well as sharing in its history, that provides a powerful element of universal appeal uniting all the diverse members.

Finally, there is the artistic dimension. Religion is supremely creative. Its very essence is one of synthesis and this dynamic has inspired all forms of creative expression. Nor is this confined to what we would now consider 'art' - an activity that has lost a great deal of meaning by being divorced from functional life. Artistic expression is just as likely to be found in the most utilitarian of sacred objects. This ranges from buildings and earthworks to sacred texts, from music, dance, and drama to gardening, the grandest ceremony to the commonest and most private act. All of these are creative manifestations, executed with care as acts of veneration and acts of communion - everyday life made sacred.

Whatever one may think of these - and one should not become too tied to actual examples - it is evident that one dimension is considered the most important. That is the dimension of experience. Without it, none of the others would have substance. It is the spark of life that lies at the heart of it all, the bright sun around which the rest must revolve.

This living heart is essential to an understanding of religion. Smart calls religion an organism. For many that would seem to be a metaphor. That may be so, but it is an apt usage that resonates with a stronger truth than mere allegory. Each religion has its own dynamic and has to be understood in terms of the interrelation of its different dimensions. But there is more to it than that. Religion and religions have life for they are an intimate part of human existence, are born out of our quest to understand the metaphysical mysteries of that existence. They would not exist without the agency of mind to create them and give them complex and evolving form, shaping what is familiar in order to express the unknown.

This is not to suggest that religions are in any way a mere invention of human beings, any more than this is a conflation of religion with the divine. Religion is a creation of human beings, not an invention - and there is a subtle difference. Invention is merely the re-arranging of already ordered things. Creation is identifying and highlighting the patterns of order in the universe or, at a more sublime level, producing that order out of chaos. Religion is a creation because it is a response to our apprehension of the divine (in whatever form we understand that most primal of forces), an identification of the order that gave form to and underlies the universe.

In this, we can find the missing element of Smart's definition. Which is that religion is our means of coping with the apprehension, knowledge, and understanding of our metaphysical existence. It is the means by which we hope to increase that knowledge and understanding. It is an organic system through which we can come to live in accord with what we learn. It is a system through which we can come to commune with the divine.

What is the Druid Way?

Whereas the definition of religion that has just been given is one based on broadly accepted ideas, the definition of the Druid Way that follows will probably be more contentious. It is derived from personal experience and it is highly likely that if you are Druid you will not agree with all that follows. That is to the good. But if you do disagree, please don't leave it at that. Work out the reasons why. In that way you will come to a more complete understanding of your own perspective. This is not an either/or competition, set in the linear context that binds us to confrontation. Even if you disagree with what follows we may both be right. We may both be wrong. We are all simply striving after the Truth.

Druids were, originally, the intellectual caste of Celtic society. They were the philosophers and judges, the poets and priests, the historians and seers, the healers and teachers. Sometimes they were royalty and even warriors. They were certainly women as well as they were men. They were not, as such, advocates of a religious doctrine called Druidry because there was no such thing. Their titles: Bard, Ovate, and Druid (or variations thereof) are in some ways loosely analogous with the academic titles of Bachelor, Magister, and Doctor. In each case, these denote succeeding levels attained after successful study. In the case of Druids, it also conferred the right to practice in certain ways within society.

For all that individuals specialized in roles that best suited their talents, Druids had a common training, their studies being undertaken in recognized schools (true Universities) run by Druids. What is more, they practised their functions within society in a recognized way, bounded by a set of principles that derived from an absolute adherence to the Truth. This was most openly embodied in a phrase that has come down the centuries to us as *an Fhírinne in aghaidh an tSaoil* - 'the Truth against the World'.

Druids today are not what Druids were. To begin with, many present day Druids are not of Celtic origin, nor do many of them have command of a Celtic language - something that is an essential marker of a culture or people. Nor are Druids considered the intellectual caste of our society. That is partly self image for the idea of an intellectual caste does not sit easily in the modern mind - especially the mind of the modern Druid - who lives in a world where the notion of intellect has been debased.

Indeed, not only has the intellectual come to be identified with the detached and rarefied atmosphere of a system of privileges, many efforts have been made to divorce it from and denigrate the use of intuitive faculties. It is a position that is bolstered only by force. Like philosophy, it is time that intellect was reclaimed and put to right use.

Intellect is the faculty of knowing, perceiving, and thinking. This does not exclude the use of intuition or creativity any more than it excludes skill with one's hands. We come to know the world through all our senses and through our interaction with the world, not by divorcing ourselves from it. You can know trees by reading about them in the classroom and thinking about them. You can know trees by climbing them. You can know trees by planting their seeds and watching them grow, by taking timber and crafting furniture. Who knows the world better, a gardener or a philosopher? It is, of course, a false question. Neither knows it better. They each know it differently. If, indeed, the gardener and the philosopher are different people.

We all have intellectual potential. We all fulfil it in different ways. In some of us it is developed to a greater degree than in others. Unfortunately, one of the major ways of developing intellect today is through formal education. The system as it exists in our society has become grossly perverted - a failing slave to the ailing master that is materialism. Our reclamation of the intellect, our training for its right use, must take place outside the mainstream.

For all that, it is important to remember that we are not the Druids of our Celtic forebears. We have a different role to play. But that does mean there is no continuity between them and us, any more than it means we cannot also fulfil the roles they once had, albeit in a new way. For example, the Druids' role as lawmakers in a society that has a well-established legal system is by no means defunct. Each Druid today lives by a code of conduct derived from being on the Druid Way. From that stance, a Druid will make judgements on things every day. Every time a Druid protests or makes a decision (even if it is only to insist on using biodegradable products or cosmetics that are not tested on animals), they adhere to personal laws and in so doing they sit in judgement on the status quo. The judgements may be personal, but the person does not stop at the epidermis. Our person is the sum of our relationships with the world. How we judge and act on those judgements has a deep and wide effect on the world - ripples on the surface, currents in the deep. We can, each of us, make a difference.

This means that the Druid Way, as we perceive and practise it today, is an intellectual activity. But it is an intellectual activity in the way that our forebears would have understood because Druids, past and present, engage with the world in all manner of ways. All that the Druid does is from an intellectual base; for all that Druids do is driven by the way in which they perceive the world and their relation to it. To be Druid is an expression of the whole being.

It also means that the Druid Way is an organism - one that functions at ever increasing levels of sophistication within society to achieve a number of exoteric and esoteric goals. These goals, and the methods by which they are achieved, are what tie modern Druids closely to their ancestral Celtic counterparts for they are one and the same, even if the emphasis differs to suit current needs. The goal is balance. The method is that of placing the Truth against the World. We will return to both concepts later on.

Underlying these bald statements are basic beliefs about the world that were held in times past by Druids. These were derived from the way that ancestral Celts saw and understood the world. For them it was second nature. This is how the world was. For us, it is something we have to reclaim. Our psychologies are different from our distant ancestors. We have been brought up in a post-Freudian society that is largely material and reductionist. It has been a dangerous flirtation with a belief in the absoluteness of humanity. It has failed.

In the first instance there was a belief in the unity of all things. This is a brave statement to make, as it has not come down to us in such straightforward form. But we can tell that it was so from the beliefs and attitudes of the Celts. They understood and accepted that the universe was a system of distinct manifestations that were facets of a unifying principle that was beyond description. Being a highly practical people they also accepted that such concerns were beyond us. Their veneration of the many gods and goddesses we know of was an expression of the impossibility of encompassing all things with the human mind. The gods and goddesses, the spirits, all were living symbols of various aspects or qualities which the divine might be presumed to have when in manifestation at our level of comprehension.

This is much more sophisticated than an animistic pantheism. They did not worship trees, rivers, lakes and wells, they simply recognized that these were special points of connection between themselves and the divine. They saw spirit in all things and knew that all things are distinct manifestations of the divine. Immanence and transcendence. Panentheism.

Accepting the unity of being means accepting that there is no such thing as lifeless matter. It also means accepting that spirit and matter are not opposites, but distinct aspects of a single reality. For ancestral Celts this was the starting from where they were. They worked with all levels of being (not just the material) in their own environment and in ways that suited their understanding of the natural world - with which they had far closer ties than we do at present.

As an adjunct to the principle of unity, there was also an understanding that there are different states within that unity. There have been many ways of describing this, but these days it is usually expressed in terms of density. Different densities have often been referred to by the symbolic use of the elements: earth, water, air, fire, and ether. Although these have been given different interpretations by different cultures, there is still a shared idea in the symbolism of different levels, planes, or worlds that interpenetrate and are interdependent, but which have distinctive basic forms.

In Celtic tradition there are a number of ways of constructing the different levels. In the *Vita Merlini* of Geoffrey of Monmouth they are expounded by Taliesin to Merlin. Although given in terms comprehensible and acceptable to a medieval audience, the text derives from older written material of the sixth century CE which itself records earlier oral traditions. All this was much later interpreted as the Circles of Abred, part of the poetic tradition of the Celts that keeps ideas alive in forms appropriate to the times.

Inherent in the notion of different states is to be found the idea of progressive development. In essence, this is the belief that there is movement from the densest most rudimentary forms of life toward the worlds of spirit and those that lie beyond that horizon. In one sense this is an acceptance of evolution, but it extends well beyond the evolution of biological form and includes the life within the form.

The idea of progression is far from straightforward. Biological evolution tends toward an increasing complexity of form and specialization of function. From this model, however, we cannot assume that complex forms or systems are necessarily superior to or more desirable than less complex forms. Complexity can lead to too great a degree of specialization, which is vulnerable to slight changes in environment. Many complex forms have become extinct whilst simpler forms have survived.

There is a lesson here for society - too great a level of social complexity can be considered a disadvantage in the evolution of social structures. This is especially so when coupled with the notion that progress simply means accumulation of material goods. Such societies are certainly more prone to catastrophic collapse. They also have a tendency to swallow less complex social structures as they expand. But less complex societies and cultures, as well as those that are not obsessed with material wealth, have a strength not often recognized.

It is also often overlooked that if biological evolution tends toward a complexity of form, its overall dynamic must favour cooperation over competition. If it favoured competition, then the trend would be toward an ever-simplified overall form. Eventually there would be a monoculture that would, by dint of its becoming the only form, die out.

Biological evolution is, however, only part of the story. The life within the form also evolves and, as it evolves, increases its capacity to evolve. Yet no matter how evolved the life in the form has become, it is only there because it has passed through all the necessary prior stages - learning from each stage the lessons that enable progress.

Our exposure to a materialistic society makes it extremely difficult to view progress as anything other than linear. It is one of the greatest differences between ourselves and our ancestors who saw things as cyclical. They existed in close communion with the natural world, were aware of the distinct and ever changing seasons. The seasons and the change of the seasons have an effect on the world about us and on our physical and spiritual being. This goes beyond the simple effects such as change in temperature, number of daylight hours, and the emotional connotations that we build up as we move through life. The cycle of change is intimately related to the cycle of change in our inner life and from this we can glimpse the many layers of the many cycles that involve the self and the other, the material and the spiritual, the tangible and the intangible.

The orthodox way of viewing our lives, for example, is as a straight line. We are born, we move inexorably through the years, we die. It is a bleak picture. True, the lines will run parallel, cross, tangle, but in the end the isolated line simply comes to an end. But this way of looking at things does not accord with people's experience of the universe, any more than it accords with the thinking of most other societies in most other times.

There is another way of viewing our lives. It is a way which lies deeply within us, usually unacknowledged, and which accords with the observable workings of the universe. Indeed, so much does this way lie at the heart of all things that it is recognized by all spiritual teachings as a primary form of existence. In our lives, at this level of incarnation, we recognize this way of looking at the universe as symbolized by the circle.

Although the circle is perhaps the simplest symbol of all in visual terms, it is infinitely complex in its representation and interpretation. The most important thing to remember when contemplating any circle is that it is not a static symbol. The circle always moves - either turning about its own centre so that the circumference rotates or pulling you into and beyond the space it contains within the circumference.

By adopting the circle as a means of symbolising our life, the connection with the rest of nature becomes apparent. The cycles of night and day, of the moon, of the seasons, all resonate one with another. More tellingly is the fact that the cycle of our life accords so closely with the seasonal cycle of the year. What we know of the Earth and the Sun, of the planets and the stars simply confirms all this.

Of course, the situation is much more complex than the mere turning of a circle. Nothing ever repeats itself exactly. In looking at the circle, we are looking at one manifestation, one cycle that turns within many others. Although each circle turns about a centre, that centre is not still for it, too, turns about another centre which, in turn, turns about another centre.

All these cycles move at slightly different angles so that although we constantly return to the familiar, there is always something slightly new to contemplate. In this way the circles become helices that turn ever on or spirals that move from or to a particular point. It is a dizzying prospect that is so vast and so complex we can never hope to understand even the tiniest part of it.

Because we cannot possibly come to comprehend the true nature and purpose of Creation in this plane of existence, that does not mean we cannot work toward that end. The path of our lives and the turning of the day and the month and the year as symbolized by the circle are outward events, manifestations through distinct agents of the cycles of life. But they are effects, not causes. They are the rim of the wheel, which has no meaning in itself, but which must be related to what lies at the hub and round which the rim ever turns.

It is this acceptance of the cyclical nature of the universe that forms the basis of a belief in reincarnation. Ancient Celtic thought on this has not come down to us in any clear-cut form. Most of what the Celts and Druids thought of this has been passed on to us by people for whom the idea of an afterlife was alien. What they made of the idea of a series of lives is evident in the incredulous tone with which they report this belief. However, there is little doubt from what can be gleaned from Celtic sources that reincarnation was an accepted part of Celtic thought.

After death, one was reborn in the Otherworld, sometimes known as the Summerland or the Land of Eternal Youth. In this world it would be a cause for celebration that the soul had passed to such a wonderful place - the forerunner of the wake. The Otherworld is a place of rest and recuperation so real to the Celts that loans and other legal contracts could be held over to be fulfilled after death. A birth into this world was a soul leaving the Otherworld for a new incarnation - a cause of mourning.

This round of reincarnation is not without point. A single lifetime is simply not long enough to learn all that needs to be learned on our journey to unity. And just as we must experience many lessons, we are allowed holidays along the way - time to rest and reflect and consider what needs to be learned next.

Nor is this confined to human beings. All life is cyclical. That we do not understand some forms of life does not mean they are exempt from the basic patterns of existence. We move round the great cycles together, our own paths intertwining with the paths of others. Humans, animals, plants, minerals, single souls and groups, nations, species, planets and stars, systems, whole galaxies. We all turn, live, die, and return in glory. We are our ancestors. We will be our descendants. What we have left behind us will be there waiting for us when we come back.

Justice is a human conceptualization of the balance inherent in the universe with the idea of free will added to the equation. Entropy is a move towards balance, a place and a time in the material plane where time and place and all the inequalities inherent in them cease to exist. Linear thinkers have trouble understanding a universe that is both cyclical and in balance. They do not understand how something that is constantly changing can be in equilibrium. But keeping balance involves completing all the cycles; it involves constant change, constant readjustment, and constant learning about new conditions.

Yet justice encompasses much more than the material world. It also encompasses much more than social and legal structures. Justice is deeply embedded in the soul - part of the matrix that gives it form. This innate sense of equity, a reflection of the balance to which the universe tends, cries out against injustice and seeks to find ways to reinstate equilibrium. It is, however, extremely difficult in this day and age not to feel helpless in the face of all that we see and hear.

Nevertheless, everything we do has a consequence. That means that it is possible to make a contribution, no matter how small, to correcting the injustices of the world. Sometimes the effect is obvious and immediate. Sometimes it is a matter of faith as the effects are difficult to see or unlikely to manifest in the near future. Indeed, so long-term are some of these effects, that they are unlikely to manifest in this lifetime. But that is the essence of Service - working to an end from which we cannot benefit.

These effects are not just external. They cannot be. We are all part of the universe. What we do affects ourselves just as readily as it affects other beings. That we must all accept the consequences of our actions within and beyond a lifetime was recognized by the Celts. Not only did they have strictly enforced social and legal codes but also, as we have already mentioned, debts and contracts could be held over to the Otherworld.

How far their beliefs equated with the Buddhist and Hindu notion of karma is difficult to ascertain, but Celts had a very strong sense of justice. This was obvious from their complex legal and social structures. However, they were well aware that justice went beyond their own social structures. Celtic justice was based on wisdom and an understanding of the workings of the world. It was based in the primacy of Truth.

The Celtic view of the world was supremely complex and subtle. It was also extremely practical. Whilst they may have happily supported an intellectual elite, they were a farming people who were concerned with winning a living from the land, who knew that a successful living was only to be had by respecting the many levels of being that permeated their own.

This view of the world and this practical approach was the basis of all Druidic thought. It is from this that present day Druids derive their sense of identity and their strength of purpose. Recognizing that their fundamental role is unchanged from that of their ancestors, but that a change of emphasis is occasioned by changes in society, they now work to learn how to restore the balances that their ancestors once worked to maintain.

Today a Druid will follow the threefold Way in likeness of an eagle, watching keen-eyed and absorbing all into their stillness; in likeness of a tree, fixing into their being all that they have absorbed; in likeness of the sun, radiating the warmth and light of all that they have learned.

By birch they work to know and preserve the history of the Druid Way and its peoples; know and protect the places of the Way; express the Way in all its forms through arts, crafts, and all the actions of their life; keep alive the traditions of the Way; seek out and preserve the ancient wisdom; uphold the freedom to right expression; learn and understand and keep the sacred word; open doors with the power of the word; be a force for good in the world.

By yew they work to know, understand, and respect the trees and their ways; know, understand, and respect the creature peoples and their ways; know compassion and, in accordance with their skills, heal the hurts of the world; converse with their ancestors; explore and come to know the Summerlands; understand the mysteries of death and rebirth; cultivate intuition; open the doors of time and there travel freely; know ways of understanding what is to be.

By oak they work to achieve authority in ritual and ceremony; understand, make, and keep right law; offer good counsel and advice; investigate and understand the universe; develop intellect; seek balance; get wisdom; teach; generate and regenerate.

These are by way of being vows that bind Druids to the work they undertake. As they stand, they are a key to understanding both the Druid and the Way they follow. Their importance merits a more detailed examination.

It is a function of Druids to preserve the history of Druids, their thought, and the peoples amongst whom Druids live. Preservation is not a simple matter. It cannot be done properly without also knowing and understanding what is being preserved. History should never be reduced to just an academic exercise. There is much more to it than that. Knowing one's history, be it personal or communal, keeping it accurate, and understanding it is essential to the maintenance of identity.

A person who loses access to their memories suffers not just a loss of identity, but also becomes rootless and lost. Without the relationships they have built up over the years with the world about them and with other people, they face many problems. The same is true of a people who lose access to their history. If that goes, so too does their identity and their social cohesion. It is one of the reasons why the cultivation of memory was so important to Druids.

Loss of identity is traumatic. There are far too many examples of how peoples have suffered when others have denied them their past. Nor can it simply be restored by regaining the facts. The ways in which a history is handed down and the ways in which it is understood are also important. Understanding a history is a restoration of the emotional facet of identity - the dynamic that vitalizes the facts.

Identity does not reside merely within a person or people, any more than it is merely about a memory of events and relationships. Nor should it be confused with individuality - a dangerously misleading notion about cutting one's self off in order to stand out.

Temporally, identity spans all time. Not only does it evolve and stand at its present juncture based on what has been, but it also exists in the moment where all its potentialities are ready to be triggered, moving as well toward possibilities that may or may not come to be. Spatially, part of the context in which identity is based is the physical environment of a person or people. That is, identity is rooted in and operating through both time and place.

It is, therefore, incumbent upon a Druid to know and understand the places that are of importance both to the identity of Druids and the people amongst whom they live. And just as history should be passed on, so too should place. We cannot freeze it, but we can cherish it and pass it on in a healthier condition than when it came in to our care. And pass it on we must, for place is not something that we can treat as if it were property. The hills and the trees cannot be ours - how can something that will outlive us belong to us? The birds and the beasts are not ours - how can something that we did not bring into being belong to us?

The idea that we cannot own the land, the flora and the fauna, but that we hold it in trust for the common good of present and future generations is not a new one. It was central to the thinking of our Celtic forebears and it helped shape the structure of their society. But this sensibility of place does have an obverse in that there is a very real sense in which we belong to the land.

This sense of place lies partly in emotional attachment. As with history or memory, emotion gives vitality to what would otherwise be a recognition of biogeographical facts. But beyond that lies the understanding that we, in common with all things, are born of the earth. Many profess this in a vague whole-earth sense - which is valid at a cosmic level - but we are all born of specific mothers as well and this finds resonance in our attachment to a specific place.

In this day and age, when most of us are born and live in an urban environment, leading itinerant lives, it can be difficult to understand the relevance of place to our way of life. We have to remember, however, that we have millions of years of evolution behind us as a pastoral species built into our being at all levels. We are, genetically, physically, emotionally, and spiritually, inhabitants of a wilderness and pastoral landscape. Urbanization is a recent, cultural innovation that has slowly gathered pace in the last five thousand years. Indeed, it is only in the last two hundred years that urban existence (with its high levels of itinerancy) has become a norm, doing much to dull our sense of place.

Yet, it is not an inevitable consequence of urban living. It is possible to rekindle a sense of place. It simply means delving a little deeper. We do not have to accept the place we inhabit at face value - even if we live in wilderness. Beneath the surface we can find much that will enable us to make contact with the spirit of a place. Even then, we may find that we do not belong, that some other place calls to us.

Anyone who is prepared to investigate an urban environment will soon find that the houses, shops, and factories are a thin veneer over a landscape as fascinating as any rural scene. Sadly we are all too often unable to see beyond the built environment - important as that is. Perhaps if we appreciated the landscape beneath, it may be that the structures we place upon it would be more sensitive - constituting a better place in which to live.

Of course, there will always be those whose roots seem to be in some place other than the one in which they were born or presently live. Not all attachments are evident or easy to discover. Some may feel rootless all their lives as they never discover this other place. For some, it is the travelling to which they are rooted. Others may discover the place and though they may never get the chance to move and settle there, simply knowing the place exists can be a source of great strength in their lives.

This awakening to a sense of place may be serendipitous, or it may come as the result of a spiritual and geographical search. To all who know it, however, there is always a sense of being at or returning to one's home - a place where we belong, where there is always a seat at the hearth, where our inner being is perfectly reflected in the landscape about us.

There are wider implications in all this because knowing and understanding place carries with it a deeper understanding of the natural world as a whole - of how we stand in relation to it, of how the actions of humanity are slowly but surely destroying the strands of the web of life that support us. And we cannot know this and do nothing about it. If we hold the land to be precious, if we accept our unity with the land, we must surely work to protect and to heal it.

Preserving, knowing, understanding, and becoming emotionally involved with the temporal and physical dimensions of Celtic and Druidic sensibilities is all very well, of course. But there is also the need to recognize that this is no game, no hobby, no weekend pastime. We are dealing with a living tradition that requires more than just knowledge or occasional flirtations with an ideal to express it.

Indeed, one of the great things about the Celtic metaphysic was that it refused to indulge in a sterile analytical, empirical, materialistic approach to life. Druids, for example, may have been the intellectual elite of their society but much of their learning, their wisdom, the genealogies they guarded, the laws they made and kept were expressed in poetry and song. The Celts were - and still are - renowned for their artistry and their exuberance. Life was not a spectator sport. It was for living.

The Druid Way, then and now, is a constant celebration of life in all things. This celebration is most obvious in distinctive forms such as artwork, craftwork, music and the like. But it runs much more deeply than that. For a Druid, life runs through all things. All things are one. This means that *all* the actions of a Druid's life are a celebration.

This may seem extreme to some, but it derives directly from that recognition of the ultimate unity of all things. Nor is it enough to say that it is so. Druids are conscious of all they do and all they think and how this impacts on everything else including, as we have already implied, the natural environment. In this lies a responsibility for all that a Druid does and thinks, all that a Druid is.

Expression and celebration can be, and often are, spontaneous eruptions of emotion. Dancing, singing, and many of the shared joys of laughter and conversation are examples of this. But it is equally possible to do these things in a measured and calm way over a prolonged period. After all, organic gardening is a perfectly valid way to celebrate one's sense of union with the natural world.

There are, of course, many ways to celebrate. Not all ways are appropriate. The ways that are chosen, along with many other aspects of the Druid Way are a matter of tradition. Tradition is a peculiar thing and the term is often misused in order to give a stamp of authority to a thing or activity that does not rightly deserve it.

A thing or activity is not right because it is traditional - it is traditional because it continues to be right. Both continuity and rightness are the keys because in its essence a tradition is a handing on, an entrustment, a teaching, not of facts or events, but of a way of doing things. A right way of doing right things.

It is clear, from a moment's thought, that this relates to the spirit rather than the letter of things - way as in direction, not as in specifics. If people stick rigidly to a practice simply because that is how it had always been done, then there would never be any innovation, never be any chance to consider whether it was any longer appropriate - or desirable. Without change things stagnate and become irrelevant. Sometimes they become poisonous cankers.

We cannot, therefore, just repeat what has gone on in the past simply because it has gone on in the past. To hand a way of doing things from generation to generation requires that what is being passed on is worthy, that it is right and relevant. In other words, it must live and grow, adapt to the times. And when it is time for it to depart, it must be allowed to go with grace.

Until that time, it must also retain its identity otherwise it mutates into something else and the tradition dies prematurely. To achieve this, a profound understanding of the Way is essential. Not only does this ensure continuity at a deep level, it provides those who practise within the tradition the courage to initiate change where it is relevant and necessary.

That is why the Druid of today is both different from his ancestors whilst continuing a recognizable tradition. Certain aspects of Druidic practice have changed to stay in concord with present circumstances. But the essence and the dynamic are the same - a tradition kept alive and handed down through the centuries.

This tradition derives from the teachings of the Druids and the metaphysic of the Celtic peoples. They considered the universe to be a spiritual entity in which all forms of life are sacred, each being, each aspect, each feature invested with a spark of the sacred. Accepting this and the fact that human life, though divine, is not special, the Celts did not try to master the universe or impose their will on others - spiritually, philosophically, or materialistically. What they sought was an inner illumination that would light the way to an ever-growing spiritual awareness in the outer world.

Much of the guidance for this is to be found in the teachings of Druids past and present. There is, of course, no accepted canon. There is not even an agreed corpus of literature, although certain texts will be found on the bookshelves of most Druids. Here, once again, it is the Truth that must be sought out. It is the task of each Druid to do this, to assimilate what they learn, and to test it in practice. That which stands the test of time tends to be preserved.

In order to do this properly, Druids have to give voice to their thoughts, just as they have to listen and respond to the voice of others. Giving voice is not restricted to speech for Druids can and do express themselves in many ways. The dialogue that ensues works at many levels, but always with the same enlightening aim.

There can, therefore, be no special licence to do and say whatever one pleases. We have a right to express ourselves freely, but the right to free expression has an integral and reciprocal responsibility to express only what is right and true.

Much that passes for right expression is badly tainted. Truth takes second place to ego in a desire to shine brighter than others, in a desire to be different, in a desire to impress. Some fall under the spell of others and speak with a voice that is not their own. Much of this sort of thing has become the norm in our media-rich world. It is easy to feel insignificant, especially where an adherence to Truth is concerned. But all this derives from a morbid desire to cut one's self off from the rest of life, as if it were somehow possible to survive without the sustenance that others provide.

The Celtic understanding of the world included a strong sense of identity with the tribe, the people. Nor was this anthropocentric, for the tribe was rooted deeply in the soil of the place it inhabited and its being was often symbolized by the adoption of an animal totem.

Being part of a tribe does not mean subsuming one's person in some slavish allegiance. Personal identity derives not from the self, but from everything around us. We are a node, a nexus, a unique point through which all about us flows. That unique point is what identifies us as distinct entities. If we cut ourselves off from all that makes us what we are, we truly become nothing.

This is a notion that many find difficult to comprehend. We have been brought up in a society that venerates the individual. The great and glittering prize of fame is a hypnotic poison. Fame for fame's sake, cults of the celebrity, are some of the more obvious symptoms of a spiritually empty life. It is one of the drugs that keep our dying society alive just a little bit longer.

Within Celtic society, within Druidic practice, the thought was to be straight and true. If what one did made one's name known, it was incidental to all else. Many object to this idea, citing the boasting of Celtic warriors as a counter example. But that, too, must be seen in the context of the Celtic metaphysic. A warrior who boasted of their prowess did nothing more than say 'what a wonderful tribe I belong to that could produce such a one as me, what a wonderful sovereign I follow, whose people could elect such a one as that to lead them'.

The voice of the Druid is a conduit for the Truth, which must be heard in the World. Further, the voice in the outer world is mirrored by the voice within the inner world. Every word, every form of expression has power. We all know this in its crudest form. Words *can* hurt. But the words used in this world to hurt someone else do nothing but hurt the one who spoke them in the inner worlds. Words used to heal strengthen the healer.

All expressions, be they made concrete or simply held in the potential of one's thoughts, are reflected in this fashion. And as the Druid works and matures, they work within as much as they do without. On the inner planes they will find that expression takes different forms, is vastly more refined, yet it still reflects in the outer world.

There, on the inner planes, are sacred words, forms of expression that contain great power. These are words that reach deep into the mysterious heart of the universe, there to resonate and ignite the great light of Truth. It is a long work of many lifetimes, the heart of the Bard's mystery, learning and understanding - knowing the word, knowing the voice that will carry the word.

As with other aspects of the Druid Way, the learning must be put to use, must serve, if it is to be truly part of the Way. That is why it is a Way. Not just a road to be travelled, but a method of travelling. A method to be shared, a Way on which to bring others. It is here that the power of the word is best put to service, opening the Way to others.

None of this is worth anything without an absolute commitment to the central tenet of the Druid Way - Truth. For some, Truth is a harsh light to face, but life cannot be lived properly without it. Be this personal or communal, the Truth is the only real measure of how we live our lives, of how right and good our part in the world has been.

Truth can be taught by many teachers. Of all that a Druid does and a Druid is, it is their connection with trees which is best known and least understood by those outwith the Grove. Even in this ecology conscious age, many still do not understand or value trees quite as they should. There is not the space here to consider this and it has, besides, been done so ably by others. Suffice it to say that we now stand so far apart from trees that most people no longer fully appreciate their fundamental role in our lives.

The ecologist and the biologist well understand their vital place in the life of the land, but only those who have depended upon trees to provide them with food and shelter know of their life and wisdom, know what it is that they might teach us if we would but slow down and learn to listen. It is not an easy task. They live at a different pace. One or two venerable sages, great and ancient yews, have been watching over us for thousands of years.

Although their wisdom is the deepest, trees are not the only forms of life that can teach us. There are those whose lives outpace our own, whose existence is sublime, and whose way through the world contains so many lessons for us we could not possibly hope to assimilate them all. Taking some cognizance of this, however, is essential to our own well-being. It is a step along the Way, coming to know the world of which we are a part from a perspective that lacks the complications of our consciousness.

What we learn from observing and listening to the life with which we share this planet is manifold. We come to appreciate our place in the web and understand the world. This understanding is one not just of seeing what is, but of feeling what is. The better we know the world, the more we enter into it, and the more we develop a fellow feeling for all other forms of life. Such compassion is essential if we are to see the balance that must be restored, the healing that must be done.

Healing is often taken to mean curing the sick, the sick being almost exclusively human. Restoration to health, however, is not simply a matter of treating the symptoms. The symptoms of the sick human point to a root cause that can be eliminated or minimized. The symptoms of the sick planet are the same. The root cause is humanity's attitudes to the rest of the world. Bring this into balance and much else will be restored. That does not mean that the symptoms should not be treated as well. Both approaches, prevention and cure, are so desperately needed at this time.

Much of that deeper healing, the restoration of a balanced metaphysic, can be derived from a wisdom that has been available to us since humans first began the great adventure that allowed them to stand within and without at one and the same time. It is a wonderful gift that we have much abused, having ventured too far away from the source of all we know. The wisdom is still there, however, a gift from those who have gone before, a gift of the few that walk amongst us still.

By far the greatest proportion of that wisdom is a legacy from our ancestors. To understand it fully, to get the best of it, Druids learn how to converse with those who have gone before. The most obvious ways of doing this is through conversation with their elders, the reading of books and documents, and the study of folkways. But there are deeper and better ways to understanding.

To converse with the ancestors is to be aware of the cycles of life and death and the mysteries that attend those cycles. Awareness and acceptance. To accept that we all will die, that the ones we love will be taken from us, is to free ourselves of the fear that many feel. Many who profess a belief in some form of afterlife seem unable to accept the fact that death is a reality of life. It is one of the most difficult things we must face.

Acceptance and the abeyance of fear do not mean that we do not and should not mourn the loss. When the emotional ties that bind us to others are severed in any way, it is always painful. True mourning is part of the healing process that restores emotional balance. But those who have gone have a journey to make, as do those of us who remain, and those journeys cannot be conducted properly if we are held back by ties in a world to which we do not belong. We can accept our own pain, but we should also celebrate the life that has passed and be happy that those we have lost are in a far better place.

By removing the obsession with a particular point on a particular cycle of our lives, we loosen the grip that time has been allowed to place upon us. This, in turn, weakens the importance that is given to a linear view of events. In doing this, we allow our intuitive faculties to emerge from the diminished shadows of analytical intellect and take their rightful place as a method of apprehending the world.

Once we come to acknowledge our existence as cyclical, once we are free of the notion of time as linear, and once we have free rein of our intuitive faculties, time becomes something to which we can open the doors and explore. The past, the future, and the present all become open to us in ways we could not have imagined.

Travelling freely in time does not automatically endow us with infallible hindsight or foresight. There are many futures just as there are many pasts. The present in which we live is where they all meet. The key lesson to learn is that our visions of the past and our visions of the future are what guide our present actions. And it is our present actions that are the most important, for it is those that validate the past as we see it and which will bring about the future that is consequent upon them.

This is vital. The future is not a foregone conclusion, a fixed point to which we are bound. That would make a nonsense of the idea of free will. It would also make a nonsense of the idea that we are responsible for our actions. The future is, in fact, an ever-changing entity that is rooted in the past and given form in the present.

What has gone before, the work of the Bard and the Ovate, provides the foundation for the Druid proper. Another turn of the circle comes. The first turn is that in which all is absorbed - the journey into the labyrinth. The second is that in which what is absorbed is fixed into form - the facing of the mysteries in the heart of the maze. Finally, is the return from the centre to face outward, radiating into the world all that has been learned.

Before giving out, however, a Druid must be certain of their own authority. This is wide-reaching in many respects, for not only must a Druid know that they are ready for this role, they must radiate that authority to others. It is a peculiarly difficult stage for many Druids to reach. Not because they are lacking in knowledge and understanding, but because attaining a high level of knowledge and understanding makes one realize how little one really knows. This is just one more turn of the circle, the master realizing they are but the humblest of pupils.

Very often the role of Druid is one that circumstance thrusts upon the person. Just as the novice finds a teacher when the time is right, the teacher finds a novice when it becomes expedient. Indeed, any person who seeks the role of teacher is unlikely to be ready for the task. When it does come, it is the beginning for the teacher as it is for the pupil.

One area where authority is important, especially in the sense of strength, is in conducting ritual and ceremonial. These are the areas where all the worlds touch, inner and outer. Many forces come into play and are focused on a particular place at a particular time. If there is not the strength to direct and channel these forces, all sorts of damage can be done.

Although the main concern is with right working with esoteric forces and with the souls and spirits of those involved, there are other important issues involved. Not least of these is the fact that ceremonial occasions are those where the Druid Way is most likely to be exposed to those outwith the Grove. What people see of the Way at these moments is of great importance.

This is not a matter of image, at least, not in the sense beloved of politicians - all surface and no substance. Nor is it a matter of ego. Yet what people see of the Way and the conduct of those who profess to follow it, are of great importance. The Druid Way is a serious and vital undertaking. Those who make it look ridiculous, those who cannot control (themselves or others), those who have not the strength or the dignity to conduct themselves well, bring the Way and its true followers into disrepute. This in turn damages the prospects of those whose search may well have led them in the direction of the Way. They may well be put off by what they see and possibly lost in this lifetime to a proper understanding of the world.

Control is a contentious issue. The Druid Way is not about having power over others. It is, however, about taking responsibility both as an individual and collectively. It is also about exercising discipline. By the time an adherent has reached the Druid grade, they are a practising Druid. In reality, learning and practice go hand in hand throughout one's life, but the more adept one becomes, the greater is the emphasis on living what one has learned.

By this stage, the transmutation of the spirit is such that one has become a new person whose every thought and action is guided by the metaphysic of the Druid Way. This requires great discipline, especially in the face of so much alluring opposition from the prevailing world view. A Druid has to govern their life in accordance with a law that they derive from their view of the world. No one else's will do.

They have to govern the life of others as well, giving advice to and counselling those who are in the early stages of following the Way. They are no longer the novice, sheltered from the world by their guides and teachers. They have in turn become a guide, a teacher, and taken on the task of bringing others into the Light. It is what being a Druid is - Service. Serving Truth. Serving the

Light. A Druid strives to become a master in order that they make a better servant of themselves.

The cycles turn and turn again. Each time the start point comes around again, everything is presented from a new perspective, seen through the eyes of experience. Much begins to fall away as the universe becomes easier to understand, more goes as understanding itself falls away and a direct communion with the universe begins to make itself felt in every last action and thought.

Here the balance is intimately felt and everything is focused on restoring and maintaining equilibrium and unity. Whilst this state of being is at the very heart of the mysteries associated with the Druid Way, it is also a return to a very simple approach to everyday life. Living lightly on the surface. Living deeply in the heart.

Even from this partial elucidation of the Druid Way, it is clear that it has distinct dimensions, just as religion does. However, where religion is seen as having six essential dimensions, the Druid Way consists in nine.

The first of these is what might be termed the tribal dimension. It encompasses the languages, history, traditions, myths, wisdom, and the geography of the people who follow the Druid Way. In essence it is everything that has to do with the identity of the tribe as well as its place in and relation to both time and space.

Then there is the dimension of craft. The term is used in its broadest sense, running from what we now call the arts (decorative and performing) through to handicrafts, domestic arts, agriculture, gardening, and, of course, all other manifest forms of magic. All of these are an outward, physical manifestation of the metaphysical stance that informs every nuance of what we do.

The next dimension is that of healing, the restoring of balance. Fundamental to this is an understanding of the world and all that is in it, on both material and spiritual levels; of the ways in which the Mother and all her children come to be damaged; and of the many ways in which each of us can best use our own skills to aid in their (and thus our own) salvation. Although Druids will treat the symptoms as and when the need arises, their major work is in re-balancing the very basics of being - healing the battered soul of the world.

The metaphysical dimension is concerned primarily with the mysteries of and reasons for being, of life and death and re-birth, of the cycles in our lives. It is also that aspect of the Way concerned with the understanding and wisdom that can be distilled from contact with our ancestors and with the Otherworld. It is exploration in this dimension that lays open the ways in which Druids see the world, the foundation of all they are and do.

Complementing the metaphysical dimension, which draws a great deal (although not exclusively) on the past, is the dimension of see(r)ing. Many assume that a seer is simply concerned with the future, but that is only part of their role. They look into the present as well which is no less obscure to us than the future might be. When the developed forces of the intuition are allowed to range across the wheel of time, nothing is irrelevant to the place and the time that is the now.

In all that goes on around us, there are times when we need to stand back from it all and make formal and measured communion. It is the dimension of ritual that defines this. But it does more than enfold the major rituals and ceremonies, the life-markers and the eight-fold cycle that celebrates the turning of the year. There are also many other private rituals and ceremonies, exercises, prayers, meditations, teachings, and disciplines involved in becoming and being Druid.

Druids are intimately involved with the world about them and there is a dimension to the Druid Way that is concerned with natural philosophy. This is the search for an understanding of the ways and workings of the world of which we are all a part; a search for an understanding of the universe.

The eighth dimension is that of teaching. Although this refers to the strict sense of teaching the Way to others, guiding them to and through the forest of the spirit, it does have a wider application. Druids engage in a constant dialogue with the world. They listen, they respond. It is part of the giving back. Often, that teaching is accomplished by example, living in a way that might inspire others to follow suit.

Finally there is the dimension of Service, the very heart of the Druid Way. The goal of a Druid is not to better their self. They all do that as a matter of course, but solely as a means to an end. To be Druid is to work to place the Truth against the World with the intent of making it a better place for all. To be Druid is to celebrate and venerate the Mother and all her children. To be Druid is to become an adept so that one can better serve.

None of these dimensions exist as separate entities. Indeed, they do not have much existence beyond these pages. They are presented here as distinct facets of the Druid Way for the purpose of this discussion, descriptions from a specific perspective. And even in this context they must be seen as overlapping, intertwining aspects that complement one another. In reality they are a unity. All is in each and each is in all.

Using this perspective is a device for comparing these dimensions with those of religion outlined earlier. And in so doing, it is easy to see that there are correspondences, both direct and indirect. All of the dimensions of religion are to be found within the dimensions of the Druid Way. None of the correspondences are exact.

Neither healing nor natural philosophy, as examples, seem to have a mainstream function within religion. That may explain why religions have so assiduously denied the connection of humanity with nature, let alone its place or purpose within it. The concern of most religions has been almost exclusively with the next life of human beings and they have been prepared to sanction the destruction of the rest of creation in achieving that.

Religion also lacks a dimension of Service in the Druidic sense. True, there are aspects of service within the social and ethical dimensions of religion, but these are tied in with the doctrinal aspects which state that right social and ethical behaviour are not only prerequisites of right religious behaviour, but also the way to get your reward in the afterlife. Service does not, however, accrete to or derive from other aspects of the Druid Way. It is not there because of doctrinal demand or to gain reward. Rather, Service is the reason for the Way's existence. Service *is* the Druid Way. The Druid Way *is* Service.

Conversely, the Druid Way has no apparent dimension of experience - which sits at the heart of religion. That is because the Druid Way is not a system that has evolved from such experience merely to codify it. This is not to deny an element of mystical experience to the Druid Way. It is there in abundance. It is simply that the Druid Way has evolved from a broader base of experience.

To be Druid is to make a commitment to the whole world both spiritually and materially. This derives from the understanding that all is one and that the actions of people interrelate with and affect the rest of the world at all levels of being. It also derives from a belief that we are endowed with free will and the concomitant responsibilities. The Druid Way is, therefore, derived not from a set of special experiences, but from all experience interpreted through the medium of the Celtic metaphysic.

We have now moved a step closer to resolving the original question. From the above we can see that there is an extremely close relationship between the Druid Way and religion. In many respects they are identical. But there is not enough there to answer the question unequivocally. To do that, there is one further point that must be touched on, as it will help to clarify the position and resolve the issue.

In 1913, the Swedish scholar Nathan Söderblom noted a distinction that is embraced by most of the world's religions - in practice if not in doctrine. He wrote, 'Holiness is the great word of religion; it is even more essential than the notion of God. *Real* religion may exist without a definitive concept of divinity, but there is no real religion without a distinction between holy and profane.' (Italics mine.)

Two words here need our consideration for they both have a number of meanings that are relevant. Holy. Profane. 'Holy' means 'sacred, pertaining to deity, held in religious awe, saintly, free from sin, pious, connected with religion'. 'Profane' means 'showing contempt for sacred things or persons, blasphemous; not concerned with sacred matters, secular; not initiated, ignorant of sacred things; wicked'. In the context of the discussion that has gone before, and juxtaposed as they are, 'holy' is used to mean 'sacred' and 'profane' is used to mean 'secular'.

Given that a Druid accepts both the unity of all things and that there is a spiritual dimension to existence, the above distinction means that the Druid Way is not a *real* religion. It cannot be. To be sacred is to be endowed with spirit. To the Druid, all things are endowed with spirit. For them, there is no profane aspect to the universe.

The thoughts and actions of human beings are another matter for they are, in the main, inventions - re-arrangements of already ordered things. Those re-arrangements can work in concord with the world, or they can be in discord. Our freedom of will allows this. By becoming a Druid, by entering the great forest of being, each person enters into a special relationship with the world, one that works to bring harmony, one that accepts the sacred in all things, one that exists to create rather than invent.

So, just where does that leave us in our quest - apart from with a large number of new questions? Is the Druid Way a religion? It all hinges on whether you can accept the distinction made by Nathan Söderblom. If the distinction between sacred and secular is one you do not accept, the Druid Way is a religion. If you do, the Druid Way is not a religion. That is, it is not a real religion.

For ancestral Celts, their metaphysic, as well as their spiritual and religious sensibilities, worked on three levels. There was what might be termed the Outer Mysteries, the commonly understood and celebrated wonders of the universe. Beyond that were the Sovereign Mysteries in which the tribe's ruler underwent tests to ascertain their fitness. Although these concerned ordinary folk inasmuch as they were to do with the prosperity of the land, they were confined to those in a position to undertake such a quest. This has come down to us in distorted form as the outer Grail quest, the restoration of the Wasteland. The third, innermost level, was a spiritual Grail quest undertaken by those of the Druid caste whose skill and wisdom led them there.

Each of these is part of the other, appropriate for their purpose. Each of these was presided over by Druids in their various roles. The Druid Way works at similar levels. It has an outer function that celebrates creation and marks its ever-turning cycles, working at a material level to conserve and regenerate the planet. Many are content with that. But often, this leads to the inner levels where an acceptance of the sacred in all things becomes a communion with the divine nature of the universe. So there is a sense in which one can embrace the outer aspects of the Druid Way without seeing it as a religion. All priests were Druids, but not all Druids were priests. Of course, if the Druid Way as described above is not a religion, then the question has to be asked - what is it?

That may not be the definitive answer to the question that you had hoped for, but that does not invalidate the exercise any more than it means we should stop exploring. When you stop, you stagnate; you never discover anything new. When you stop, you have nothing that is yours that really matters enough to pass to your children - something that will allow them to move deeper into the forest, closer to the Grove. It is important, therefore, to discuss all things carefully and extensively, knowing that the best we are going to do is move closer to the answer, nearer to the Truth. We are not going to reach it.

Indeed, it is not every question that has an answer. It is not everything that is open to proof. However necessary philosophical proof may be in some areas, it cannot ever be sufficient to define religion, the mysteries, or the Druid Way. After all, one of the basic tenets of all these is to accept - accept the validity of our experiences and accept that others can and do share those experiences in some form or other. It means we have to take some things on trust. Accepting, walking into the abyss (as does the Fool of the Tarot) is part of being Druid.

Accepting is not, of course, the same as acquiescing. Accepting that there is evil does not mean we must not fight against it. Accepting the divine does not mean that we should not enquire after it in order to achieve a deeper understanding. The only thing that should go unquestioned is that we Serve, placing the Truth against the World. And to do that, we must ever seek to come closer to knowing just what Truth might be.

TRUTH AND SERVICE

In the previous chapter, the saying 'the Truth against the World' was used on several occasions. It is, for some, a contentious phrase. For that reason, along with a number of others of equal importance, it is one that deserves our close consideration. Meditation on its meaning takes us to the heart of what it means to be Druid - what a Druid is, what a Druid does, the way in which they conduct their lives on both the outer and inner planes of their being.

This is not to say that the interpretation of the phrase that is offered here is the 'correct' one. There is and can be no 'correct' interpretation. It is simply used here as a way of illuminating certain elements that are essential to the Druid Way.

It was also stated in the previous chapter that the Druid Way is Service. This, too, deserves further consideration. It is all too easy to become engrossed in thinking about what it is to be Druid without ever thinking about *why* it is a Way that you have chosen, why it is a Way that is chosen by an increasing number of people.

The question 'Why?' is one that adherents of any faith would do well to ask. Sadly, it is a question that is rarely encouraged. It all too easily rocks the shaky foundations on which dogma is constructed. It all too easily exposes the power structures that have grown about the original inspiration in a smothering accretion of hypocrisy.

Of course, the answer has a great deal to do with where a person was born as much as any other factor. Environment is important in influencing choice. It is also important in shaping the person who makes the choice. Whatever its influence, however, it is rarely recognized or accepted as a factor.

But choice is not a given. If you were born in Britain, for example, you are far more likely to have a choice about the Way you choose to follow. Although this is, nominally, a Christian country, that has never been much more than a political facade.

Pagan ways are still strong and are evident in all areas of life - just there below the surface. The freedom of expression that goes with that, along with a multiplicity of choice and example provided by a culturally and ethnically mixed society, means we are privileged to have the opportunity to explore our spiritual being. Anyone who is born in Tehran or Rome, Antananarivo or Salt Lake City is likely to have had their path chosen for them at an age that prevents the development of an open mind. It takes a particular kind of strength and courage to break away from a path presented as the 'true way' and find another when one has been indoctrinated from birth.

Even within Britain there are places where the choice is not so free, or if freely made it cannot be openly declared. There are Druids who live in view of where this was written who know that if their neighbours were given the slightest hint they were anything other than good 'Christian' folk (of the right sect) they would be in danger of physical violence. In the face of that sort of threat, or worse, people still follow the Way that their heart and spirit crave after. To know *why* is of great importance, to all of us.

Such a question may seem to some to be unconscionably vague. But we are not after an unequivocal answer. It is not that sort of question. The point is not to find an answer, but to discuss the issues that are raised. In so doing, we help ourselves to see more clearly our purpose; we make it easier to see how we might Serve. After all, the what and the why of the Druid Way are so closely interlinked that you cannot be too far detached from one in a discussion or realization of the other.

There are, of course, numerous ways in which any of us can Serve. Many of them are not unique to the Druid Way. What makes these forms of Service into uniquely Druidic practice is their specific combination - that and the spirit or moral force that inspires them. But that is to anticipate the argument. Let us step back to the first purpose of this chapter, which is to consider what we might mean by placing the Truth against the World.

An Fhírinne in aghaidh an tSaoil - the Truth against the World. The earliest extant expression of this saying is to be found in one of the versions of the *Audacht Morainn* (the Will of Morann Mac Cairbre, a 1st century *breitheamh*), the oldest surviving copy of which is part of the *Leabhar ma Nuachongala* which was compiled around 1150CE. As far as the authenticity of the content of any early text can be established, the pedigree of the phrase can be considered reasonably strong. It is certainly not, as some have claimed, an invention of one of the 18th century revivalists - an enigmatic group who hold a curious position in the affections (or otherwise) of present day Druids.

Whatever its antiquity, we can be certain it is a genuine reflection of the importance in which the concept of Truth was held in pre-Christian times. A *breitheamh*, more commonly known now as a Brehon, was a judge, one who had the authority to investigate as well as sit in judgement on a dispute or infringement of the law. Truth was paramount in such situations and those entrusted with seeing it upheld were likely to have a deep understanding of what it meant in its broadest sense. The Brehons and the Laws they kept originated, in all likelihood, with the Druid caste.

The phrase in question has appeared over the centuries in a number of variations. All are deliciously ambiguous. Naturally, its ambiguity makes it difficult to pinpoint its meanings, but that very quality is what makes it such an excellent teaching device. In working to unravel its many possible interpretations, we are forced to explore ideas and the conjunction of concepts that we might otherwise disregard. What is more, no exploration will ever provide a definitive explication. It cannot simply be explained and forgotten. We all bring our own experience, thoughts, and traditions of thinking to its elucidation. It therefore stands good for all time as a means of enabling us to look at Truth, the World, and how these two might stand in relation to one another.

As with many such abstract concepts, Truth is not something that lends itself easily to anything like a comprehensive definition. And as anyone who has studied philosophy for long enough will know, the more complex any attempt at a definition for Truth, the less comprehensible it becomes and the further it strays from reality or usefulness.

Abstract as the concept of Truth may be, it must be defined simply and be in accord with the world if it is to be of use. And it must be of use. If it is not anchored in the reality of our being and experience, if it cannot guide us and reflect what we are and know, then it fails us at all levels.

Truth has to be felt in the heart as much as it needs to be understood in the head, something that requires us to cultivate a sensitivity to what is about us that is increasingly uncommon in today's world. Isolationism and ignorance are ever more commonplace at all levels of experience. The electronic communication revolution might have made it easier to send information, but it has actually increased the distances between us in terms of understanding.

Furthermore, Truth is sensitive to time and place. It is relative, dependent upon the metaphysic from within which it is being expressed. This is not to say that there are no universal aspects, things upon which all people agree, but Truth as we experience it is not absolute. This makes it both subjective and objective at one and the same time - a notion many of us have been taught to reject by the metaphysical orthodoxy of our culture.

Several major areas of philosophical theory concerning Truth have emerged in recent times. Correspondence theory, for example, which is widely held by some to represent a 'common-sense' view, asserts that a statement is true if it corresponds to a fact. This, of course, rests largely on our understanding of what constitutes a fact and ignores the circularity inherent in the theory - that most facts exist solely as statements. After all, even a simple statement like 'the sky is blue' is fraught with problems. If the sky is blue, then the statement is true. But the whole thing is self-referential. The blueness of a thing called sky rests far more in our perception and description of it than it does in any independent and objective factors.

Coherence theory was proposed in order to avoid this problem by internalizing it. It asserts that statements are only partly true or false, to greater or lesser degree, as Truth is essentially a system of wholeness in which the internal coherence of sets of propositions is the key factor. In other words, the more a given set of statements relate to one another and logically support one another, the more they can be said to be true. Of course, as any student of logic will tell you, it is entirely possible to have a coherent and mutually supportive set of statements that bear no relation to anything we might consider to be the Truth, let alone the real world.

Both theories fail. Whilst facts may be true, whilst statements may be coherent, something that is true does not necessarily constitute Truth in a wider understanding of what the word means. Truth can reside in fiction, in poetry, in nonsense, in art, in music, in a landscape, in an emotion, in a dream.

In keeping with the soulless traditions of modern philosophy, there is also Pragmatic theory, an application of Utilitarianism. This asserts that the truth of a statement should be measured by the consequences of its declaration. The more fruitful the consequences, the truer the statement must have been. Reprehensible as such a theory is, being devoid of justice and ethical considerations, it is the basis by which modern politics is conducted.

There are a number of other theories, but they tend to be variations on or combinations of the above. None of them are satisfactory, not least because they fail to relate to the everyday experience of people or connect with the lives they lead. But they also have a much more important failing. In common with what most of us think, Truth as a concept is all too often connected solely with language.

In our literature-rich society it has become far too easy to fall into the trap of assuming the written and spoken word to be the sole arbiters of our fate and the fount of all things. All the theories mentioned above, and the many variations thereof, are essentially about language. But Truth is not something that can be limited to language. Indeed, language is just a small part of the realm of Truth, for Truth is to be found throughout the much wider world of our being. It applies to our actions, to our behaviour, to our thoughts, to all the ways in which we live our lives and to all the places in which we live them.

In fact, it takes little enough thought to realize that language is particularly ill suited as a medium by which to express Truth. Not only is it all too easy to use language to create plausible falsehoods, but it is also a medium that is capable only of limited expression of human experience. If we confine discussion and understanding of Truth solely to language, then we restrict ourselves to a system that poorly reflects the world.

Language is essentially a two-valued (a word is used or it is not used; it is used correctly or it is used incorrectly) and linear medium over which most of us exercise limited command. It is used to convey information about the world, which is multi-valued, non-linear, and saturated with information. Too much emphasis on language leads to people trying to make sense of reality through an inadequate means of expression. It is akin to a single monochrome pencil sketch, made by someone who is not skilled at drawing, being used to represent the visual, aural, and emotional content of a full-colour motion picture. It can be done, but it is very far from adequate.

Unfortunately, for all the claims that we are becoming less literate, the emphasis on language has become inevitable in our culture. It has made itself so. Too great an emphasis on acquiring the skills of alphabet literacy at too early an age actually biases our thought processes, developing one side of the brain to the detriment of the other. This is not an irreversible process, but it is one that is little understood, and buried deeply away from casual enquiry. Much of the contemporary Western metaphysic is rooted in this bias.

That is why those who seek a new way of looking at the world often find it necessary to break away from the printed word, from visual media (itself based on the printed word and the linear narrative forms derived from language), even from other people. Walking barefoot and alone in the forest without the need to codify the experience for the benefit of others opens up a whole new perspective on the universe, one not distorted by words or the need to organize experience in a way that can be conveyed to others. The Mystic apprehends Truth, but the mystical experience is notoriously difficult to convey to others.

This should not be taken as an attack upon literacy. The alphabet and its analogues, along with reading and writing, are all marvellous, magical gifts. But literacy is something that should be seen in perspective and treated with greater respect for what it is and what it can and, more importantly, what it cannot do.

If, recognizing the limitations of language, we consider Truth in a much wider context, it then becomes necessary to reconsider certain definitions. Truth itself has to apply to and derive from *all* things, taking on many extra dimensions that expand it from a narrow notion of the verity of language to one that applies to the rightness or fitness of a thing, any thing, all things, in whatever form they exist or are made manifest. This certainly applies to spoken and written statements, but it also includes actions, constructs, thoughts, emotions, places, and ideas. Notions of falsehood must then take their shape from this.

Suggesting that Truth is, in its widest context, something to do with the rightness or fitness of a thing is not simply plucking an idea out of thin air. It is based on the metaphysic of our Celtic ancestors, who held that all things are connected, part of a whole. To them, this was the natural order of things. The universe was just that - a uni-verse (derived from the Latin *versum unus* - which means 'in the direction of unity').

Although they recognized the distinction between such things as politics, agriculture, social culture, spirit, art, craft, this world, the Otherworld, language, action, thought, ideas - or any other such notion that we try to cram into inappropriate and often false pigeon holes - they did not separate them. Farming, for example, was just as much a matter of spirit and politics as it was of soil fertility, crop rotation and good husbandry. All life was one, each a facet of the whole, each investing and illuminating the others with a complementary energy. It still is, no matter that we do not behave as if it were. Nor did our ancestors separate their actions, their being, and the rest of the universe although, again, they well understood the distinctions between them - and in understanding the distinctions they also understood the fundamental connections.

At a superficial level this may seem like Coherence theory writ large. It is not. There is an immense difference between Truth residing in the coherence of sets of statements which may all be falsehoods and a recognition that Truth is a measure of the degree to which something is rightly integrated with the underlying unity of all things.

If we take that unity to be implicit, then Truth and Reality are necessarily isomorphic. Indeed, in some Celtic languages, Truth and Reality are denoted by the same word. Yet it is not just a matter of identifying different aspects of the universe by referring to them with a single word. The fact is, these are not different aspects. We are dealing with one thing seen from different perspectives.

Many of the problems we face today arise, in great part, from our continual and frenzied seizing upon distinctions and perspectives and trying to separate them out from unity. We have turned our back on the forest and we have become obsessed with individual trees, with the parts of individual trees. It has become an almost pathological behaviour - a behaviour that is, ultimately, both fruitless and destructive. Such greed, born of a materialistic metaphysic, extends now to all things, even to the very DNA that patterns the material form of each being. To think that this can be separated out and owned is either ignorance or it is an arrogance that is breathtaking in the extreme.

The distinctiveness of a thing lies not in the thing itself. It lies in the way we choose to look at the world. A particular way of looking will highlight specific things. What we look at, however, is always the same and underlying whatever we see, underlying that which distinguishes one thing from another, is the fact that they are all an integral part of some larger unity. The facet of a jewel does not exist without the jewel. There is no thing in the universe that is separate. That would, after all, be a contradiction of terms.

So, for a person to say that they want to pursue nothing but a spiritual path is to ignore the fact that the spirit does not exist in isolation. We live in a material universe, not to escape from it but to better understand it. Our work here is to integrate spirit and matter more fully and concordantly. After all, even the most dedicated member of a monastic community spends a large part of their waking life engaged in the physical work necessary to provide the basics of material life. This is not just so that they can maintain themselves sufficiently to pursue the spiritual life, but because the physical work *is* the spiritual life.

This also holds for a person who declares that they want nothing to do with politics. That is impossible. Politics is about the way in which we order our priorities in respect of the resources necessary to the maintenance of our being - be that material, spiritual, communal, or personal. Our every action is political and has resonance in the community in which we live. Even if we shun human contact, we have no choice but to live in communion with the rest of the world. And if we accept the unity of all things, if we accept the spirit in all things, we cannot stand by and do nothing while the world continues to be so viciously abused.

And the same is true for the person who says they simply wish to pursue and develop their cultural interests. These do not exist in a vacuum. The culture of a people consists in their political and spiritual being and how that is made manifest in the material and non-material conduct of their lives as individuals and as a community.

Many more examples could be given. The point being made is that each facet relies on the existence of all others for its own being and shape. None of them exist in a void, but are the product of all the others. And underlying all - politics, spirit, culture, art, this world, the Otherworld, language, action, thought, ideas, along with all the other diverse facets of the universe - weaving them inextricably together are the patterns and relationships that constitute what some call the natural order and others call the laws of nature.

Understanding and working in concord with those patterns and relationships to achieve some particular right end is what Druids do. It is something that is also sometimes known as magic - quite unlike the usual 'supernatural' ascription that attaches to this activity. Indeed, the whole notion of a supernatural world existing in addition to the natural world runs counter to the belief in the unity of all things. The things we refer to as supernatural are not above, beyond, or somehow outside of nature. They are all part of the natural order. It is just that they are at a level we do not yet properly understand and that some will always refuse to recognize.

This may seem something of a diversion, but that is not the case. Magic and Truth not only have a great deal in common, they are also strongly connected. For Truth is also about understanding and working with those patterns and relationships that underlie and bind the many facets of the universe into a whole. Indeed, Truth and magic might often be one and the same thing.

If we were to look for a distinction, what we would find are two aspects of the underlying principle of the universe. Magic is the right working with that principle. Truth is the right measure of that principle. That is, magic is when we understand the rightness or fitness of a word, an action, of behaviour, of the way we live, and use that understanding to achieve some right desired end. Truth is the degree to which the word, the action, the behaviour, the way we live is in accord with the underlying patterns of the universe. The distinction is subtle, but is between the inherent property of a thing and its potential to bring about some other thing.

Of course, it is all well and good talking about the universe and the natural order that lies beneath it, but it is important to know just what is meant by the phrase 'natural order'. More specifically, we need to be clear what is meant by the word 'nature', especially when it is used in conjunction with the activities of humankind, for it is the human realm that concerns us most in this particular discussion. It is also worth bearing in mind that 'universe' and 'world' are interchangeable, both terms meaning the totality of things.

We certainly cannot use 'nature' to mean 'the world as it would be if untainted by outside influence' because the world is, by definition, everything. There can be no outside influence. Nor can we satisfactorily put it in opposition to something we might call human activity because no matter how harsh that activity might be, it is the product of a species that is part of nature.

What we need is a borderline that exists somewhere within the field of human activity. Though part of nature, we are no longer wholly bound by the natural order. What is more, it is apparent from even a casual study of the world about us that some, if not many, of the things people do are actually causing the break down of the natural order. Indeed, in some cases we are beginning to see an assault on nature itself. Of course, we can and have caused breakdowns in the natural order without forethought and without intention. The first cities turned the fertile areas around them to desert. Equally, there are many people who have, by design, left no material footprint behind them to spoil what they temporarily inhabited.

It would be best, therefore, if the borderline we seek was drawn between those things we do by instinct and those that we do by choice. The reason for this is simple. We cannot alter, from one day to the next, what we do by instinct. Those are things that arise from an evolved behaviour; an unconscious following of what has been bequeathed us by the natural order. We are not, however, creatures of instinct alone.

Many of our instinctive behaviours have been traded over the millennia for learnt behaviours. Through these we have been endowed with free will. Our learnt behaviours are something over which we *do* have control - we can choose the degree to which we exercise them, we can choose between them, we can choose not to use them at all. But as well as choosing, as well as having a much wider scope than mere instinct would allow, we also have a consciousness of the world and of what we do in it. Which means we are fully aware of the consequences of what we do or choose not to do. That combination of control and awareness means that the consequences of our actions are our responsibility and ours alone.

What we do by conscious and informed choice, be that in concord with nature and the natural order or not, results in what will be referred to hereafter as the World. It is that which is distinct from nature and the natural order. It is that over which we have control. It is that alone for which we have to answer.

Most of the planet today might be called the World as the direct and indirect marks of humanity are to be seen and felt almost everywhere. Earth, air, water, even fire, all have been moulded to and by the uses of humanity ever since the first tools were fashioned. This process has continued for several million years.

As few as two thousand years ago, however, the World had barely had an impact on the planet. The majority was still wilderness, and having knowledge of wilderness as something in its own right and easily distinguished from and untouched by the areas altered and cultivated by the hands of humans was far easier then than it is today. It was more or less possible to use the word 'natural' in the sense of 'untouched by humanity' and compare that with the World made or altered by humans. It was in that climate that the Celtic metaphysic and the teachings of the Druids first found expression.

There was another important difference in the past. Not only was the World of humanity much smaller and more easily defined, but the interface between the World and the rest of the universe was a soft, amorphous thing decided upon by humanity and the universe in equal measure. This was partly because humans were not in a position to wreak mass havoc upon the universe, but it was also because humans would have had no desire to do so.

They had learned from, understood, and worked with the universe to whatever degree they were able. In so doing, they had come to know what the universe was, respect it, understand the wisdom inherent in it, and know its importance as a unified entity. Without its support, they knew, we all perish.

Today, now that the World has expanded to engulf the planet, the interface between World and universe has become sharply defined. That sharpness takes no account of the universe. It is a brutal and arbitrary thing, its position decided upon solely by human beings - most of whom would not even know the voice of the universe if they heard it, let alone understand what it has to say.

The interface between the World and the universe is far more complex, however, than most people realize. It is not a barrier, but the sum of those things that distinguish what is the World from what is not the World. It is a living organism that requires careful oversight and sensitive management. It is a conversation between interpenetrating entities in which each must listen carefully and take into account the needs of the other if one is not be destroyed.

We have grown away from the instinctive behaviour that originally governed this. We have grown away from an understanding of our place as part of the whole and thus our base level of concord with the rest of creation. Deprived of the instinct to work in concert with the universe, and ignoring the facts about our place within it, the World we are now creating is both destructive and increasingly beyond our control.

The upshot is, we no longer manage our place in the universe. We have turned our back on it, we pretend it does not exist. And where we cannot ignore it, we pretend it is of no importance. Not only is this a gross insult to the universe, it is self-destructive in the extreme. What we have turned our backs on is the larger part of our own being. And in so doing we have increased the level of our ignorance of all things.

It is an ever-increasing problem. Management of our place, knowing the relationship, understanding the interface, requires of us all a profound understanding of the workings of the universe as well as of the World. And not just an analytic understanding of the material parts of existence. That is as partial an approach as denying our connection to the natural order.

This is not to argue that the World is necessarily a bad thing. It is, but it need not be. What we are as creatures makes our position in the universe inevitable. But the form and effects of that position are *not* inevitable. We could have all the genuine benefits of the World - shared equally with all - without the current drawbacks and the dangers. But that can only be achieved through a radical change in the way we view the world.

Ancestral Celts had a much more acceptable and concordant metaphysic. The Druids understood that. They were lovers of wisdom, judges of rightness, seekers out of Truth, constantly measuring and assessing the World. It is a task faced by Druids today as well - in a world more artificially complex than our ancestors faced, a world falsely and dangerously divided. Which means that those who follow the Druid Way must know and understand the universe and the patterns and relationships on which it is based. It also means they must know and understand the workings of the World. They cannot turn their backs on it and follow their own fantasy.

To know and to understand what is about us and within us and that of which we are a part, we have to shed many notions about ourselves and the World - notions bequeathed us by centuries of an ever-evolving yet fallacious Western metaphysic. It is a developing metaphysic that is based on a flawed notion of the scientific, of analytical materialism. It is a metaphysic that embraces what we have made of the World, considering it to be an inevitability. It is a metaphysic that shuns the universe, imagining it to be a hostile place.

The universe is not hostile, however, any more than it is cold or savage. The World is neither predetermined nor necessarily a place of conflict. These ideas, so beloved of the Darwinians and their predecessors, have long since been shown to be false. They are nothing but a sad anthropomorphization of the ways in which some people would like things to work, presenting a picture of a World and a universe over which they would have control. It is a false picture, just as their metaphysic is false. Scientific materialism is nothing more than a shabbily constructed excuse for the vile behaviour that has been unleashed on the universe and for maintaining the World in which we now live.

Savagery is an attribute only of those who can choose their behaviour. Only humanity has that choice. The same is so with good and evil. These are not part of the natural order other than that they are inherent in the free will possessed of human beings. They are things we choose - which makes them an integral part of the World. They are manifestations of our rational existence and of our intentions - which makes them our responsibility and ours alone.

The universe cannot, by its very nature, be savage any more than it can either be good or evil, competitive or co-operative. It is true that the universe is a movement toward unity and that many of its facets do work in concord toward complex, climax forms, but this is inherent in the laws of nature. It is what the universe is, not what it has chosen or chooses to be, not what it has had imposed upon it from without. The weft, for all its complexity and beauty, for all the multitudinous variations that flourish, can only exist within the framework provided by the warp of all being. The universe *is* - a pure state that many mystics aspire to.

Of course, the solution to our problems does not lie simply in gaining knowledge of the universe and discovering the underlying patterns, divining the Truth. If that were so, we could each retreat and lead very satisfying lives contemplating the universe and the World. But we can't. If we tried, we would still be sitting in a haze of smug glory as it all came apart around us.

Knowing and understanding simply provides the raw material with which to work. Whilst the universe *is*, the World is distinguishable from it by the fact it needs consciously chosen actions to maintain it. The World, therefore, must be taken into our hands and our hearts and we must use the knowledge and the understanding we have of them to bring about change, to restore balance. A Druid must act in order to bring the World as close as possible to a model of non-action. That operation is real magic.

The ability to work real magic is what all Druids train for. It is a great and terrible gift fraught with many dangers, but it is a gift open to us and it is one we cannot ignore. Yet even that is not enough. There are many paths to knowledge and understanding. There are just as many ways of working with that gift and making change. After all, knowing and understanding plants, soil, weather patterns, and the like gives us the ability to garden. But having the knowledge does not make a thing so. The knowledge has to be applied - and it has to be applied in right fashion.

Indeed, knowledge and understanding are quite meaningless unless they *are* applied. This can be interpreted in two ways. It could be argued that there can be no such thing as purely abstract knowledge. All knowing is simply a facet of practice, just as all practice is a facet of knowing. Yet even if it could be proved that there were such a thing as purely abstract knowledge, one is forced to ask what its purpose might be, what meaning it could possibly have.

There are layers and directions, too, to the practice that we derive from knowledge. Just as there are gardens that give joy and maintain life in great abundance, there are also gardens that poison and destroy - maintained by the use of genetically engineered plants, fed with chemical mixes, and regularly doused with poisons. For all that knowing and understanding the universe enables us to work with its principles, for all that we actually go out and work for change, it is our values that determine in what way we should work as well as the sort of changes to which we aspire.

The Druid Way is an espousal of a specific set of values divined from an extremely ancient lineage of wisdom. It unquestionably predates the ancestral Druids, who assuredly knew its worth. They worked with it and refined it to suit the age in which they lived. And through all the ages, the underlying values have remained unaltered. It is those values that form the framework of what Druids do today.

Broadly speaking, the values in question are concerned with the restoration and maintenance of order. This is not some reactionary stance. A true understanding of the universe will show that the one constant is change. Nothing is ever still; nothing remains fixed - no matter how things may appear to us in each of our short spans of cognizance. Restoring and maintaining order means understanding the ever-evolving principles that form the universe and ensuring that everything we do adheres to and maintains these principles.

This is not in some ill-defined esoteric sense. Druids, for all that their work is largely spiritual, are rooted firmly in the World. Their heads may be in the clouds, and rightly so, but their feet are rooted deeply in the earth. It is how they maintain contact with and act as a conduit for the energies represented by the four elements.

The role of a Druid is to come to know what is Truth and consequently to work to ensure that the World is moved forward increasingly in accordance with it. Yet it goes much more deeply than that. It is not a role that can be cast off. It is what defines a person as a Druid - undertaking that mission from the perspective of a Celtic metaphysic. No easy task. Indeed, it is a demanding role and many that set out on the Way fail to appreciate that being Druid is just that - being.

Truth is the ultimate standard to which the Druid aspires. The World is their work. That work, at whatever level it is done, is Service. Truth and Service, therefore, are inextricably linked - one the active mode of the other. And if they are so linked, if everything a Druid does is directed toward ascertaining and proclaiming the Truth, then the Druid Way *is* Service.

For ancestral Druids, Service was ultimately concerned with maintaining an existing balance - materially, socially, and spiritually. Celtic society was highly developed in all areas. And whilst it was not perfect, it was more highly attuned and far more just than most societies and cultures today. The work of Druids was about defining boundaries, listening to the voice of the universe, and guiding others with the knowledge, understanding, and wisdom that they gained from the many years of rigorous training they underwent.

Today, Service has a different emphasis. It is about restoring the balance that once existed after centuries of abuse have all but destroyed it - showing that there are boundaries, showing that the universe has a voice that must be heard, showing that there are better paths to tread. And although the tasks differ, the measure is the same. Truth.

Absolute Truth is well beyond our comprehension. We might glimpse its form in and through particular instances of Truth because they are examples of the Absolute at work. These examples reveal a pattern that works just beyond our normal perceptual level - a pattern that is the essence of mystical experience. It is tantalisingly out of everyday reach, yet the glimpses are sufficient for us to work with it and understand it at an intuitive level.

Seeking out the Truth, be it a reaching for the Absolute or a working with particular instances, enables the Druid to right action. Right action has two essential elements. To begin with, it must be in concord with natural law. The means to an end must be in harmony with the end, otherwise the enterprise fails before it begins.

The other essential element of right action is that the end must not be personal. Right action might benefit those who undertake it, but that must not be the goal - otherwise it is not right action. If you grow vegetables organically, you should do it because it is in concord with the universe and beneficial to wildlife. You still get tasty and wholesome vegetables. The difference is that the means by which you achieve that end are in harmony with natural law and increase the degree to which unity is achieved.

This is a difficult concept to grasp in a society given over to a superficial adulation of the individual. Service is selfless. If not, it is not Service. Druids are selfless. If not, they are not Druids. What they are and what they do is detached, sacrificial (an action which makes sacred), and non-violent. And through the detached vision of Service, the Druid is enabled to see Truth (of all kinds) much more clearly.

The tribal life of ancestral Celtic peoples made the task easier. Service was part of everyday life for everyone. When the welfare of the group is as important as - if not more so because it supports - the welfare of the individual, working and providing for others is quite natural. Right action is normal, everyday practice.

This is especially so in a culture with a metaphysic that regards the universe as cyclic rather than linear. In a cyclic system, 'means' and 'ends' become intimately connected - the nature (the how, the why *and* the what) of one residing in the nature of the other. Our own linear, dualistic thinking has no place within it for such open fluidity. 'Means' and 'ends' are no longer considered to be related in any but a mechanistic and linear form, stripped of any meaning beyond 'cause' and 'effect'.

As so often stressed, the Celtic metaphysic is but one of many ways of viewing the universe. The Truth that is observed through this metaphysic may appear relative to Truths observed in other ways. Yet if they are genuine, then they all derive from the Absolute. Of course, Absolute Truth is largely closed to us. It is certainly beyond our empirical grasp and it is a waste of time trying to find it that way. We cannot prove it. We cannot reason it. We must learn to know it in our hearts.

As the Absolute is closed to us, we must work through the beacons of relative Truth, allowing them to guide us. Dealing with relative manifestations can bring its own problems if we are not forever aware of their relative nature. To understand and work with Truth it is necessary also to Serve, to be selfless, detached, to know one's self. Knowing one's self, knowing and acknowledging all our faults and foibles, allows us to compensate for them and judge to what extent they make Truth both relative and subjective. *We* are the glass that distorts. If we know the flaws, we can compensate and get closer to a true picture. The more we Serve, the more we understand our flaws, the more we understand Truth. A continuous cycle of enlightenment.

These are all grand sounding sentiments. Questing for and knowing the Truth; understanding the universe; Service. Of course, we can never hope to achieve these things fully in a single lifetime. Just as we can never hope to change the World overnight. What we can do is take steps towards the ultimate goals we set ourselves - steps that we can manage, steps that make a small but definable difference to the World.

Whilst we work toward these goals, we must acknowledge a number of things. We must accept that we do not know very much and that what we do know is far too much of the wrong sort of thing. We must also accept that for all the little that we do know, we understand far less. And for all that we know and understand things, our emotional development is still that of young children - stuck in the playground, playing our games and squabbling our stupid squabbles. Knowing and accepting that is also part of knowing who we are, part of knowing where we are.

In addition, we must accept that we belong, that there is a purpose. We do not tread a lone path any more than we need wander aimlessly. Every step we make affects everything around us, even the very soil on which we stand. Like it or not, we are a part and we can do nothing that has no consequence. We are each a very small facet of the great jewel that is the universe. We are connected and we have a part to play.

The part we play, the Service we undertake, cannot be fully engaged in until we each have some idea of the present state of the World. To come to that understanding we must measure the World against a standard. As we have seen, the standard by which we measure the universe is Truth. The World is part of the universe and must, therefore, submit to that same measure.

Placing the Truth against the World - that is, measuring the conscious creations of humanity against what we know of the underlying principles of the universe - reveals to us that the World is a miserable failure. Indeed, if Truth really were told, the World is an unmitigated and bloody mess. Humanity has little or no integrity. It constantly ignores or is forced to ignore the real cost of its actions. No longer listening to the voice of the universe from which the World is derived, humanity has lost control of its great construct, can only watch as its actions fail to stem the destructive monster it has let loose upon itself and the rest of creation.

To many that will sound unnecessarily gloom laden. Many people reading this will think to themselves, 'What of all the progress we have made?' But think. Progress? What progress? On what terms? Those of the scientific materialist? Don't be too quick to judge humanity by the best it might achieve in material terms. Look carefully at its record and judge it by the worst it has already done - materially and spiritually.

This is not to say there is no hope, any more than it means that good is not being done. It simply means that there is so much more to do. Which is why we need to know what we are doing and why. Without the guidance offered by the Druid Way and the Celtic metaphysic on which it is based, without the many other genuine spiritual traditions, there would be no distinctive way forward. We would be left floundering, making lots of noise and accomplishing nothing.

Even with such as the Druid Way to provide strong guidance, the task before each Druid seems daunting. But we are each capable of changing things for the better, each in our own way. Finding that way is one of the quests a Druid undertakes as they learn the basic teachings of their tradition. And, as with the quest for Truth, it is not just a cerebral exercise conducted on the inner planes of being, it is also an outer quest to achieve right action.

The personal circumstances of a Druid must, of course, be one of the prime factors in deciding how they can best be of Service. They can only start from where they are. They can only work in the World as it is. For some, making an open statement of their beliefs and showing others what this means is the best way to do this. Working quietly, perhaps alone, can achieve results equal to those who work in groups or in the public eye.

Whatever a person's circumstances may be, and however those circumstances might dictate the way in which they work to restore balance and heal the planet, the overall aim is to bring about a lasting spiritual impression with minimal hint of a material impression; to make the work easier for future generations and leave no scar at one's passing.

Such work is hard and at times a burden almost too heavy to bear. But Druids are part of a tradition that has immeasurably ancient roots and which will flourish for millennia yet to come.

They hold the line. And, as they work, ripples will flow across the surface and currents will run in the deeps of their lives and relationships with others and the planet - connecting with Truth and, through Service, spreading its influence throughout the World.

ME/NOT ME - A SEARCH FOR IDENTITY

To be Druid and work in the World is not an easy path to tread. The World is a dangerous and distracting place, erected on shaky foundations and maintained by violence. To walk there in right fashion without getting lost, either materially or spiritually, requires a great deal of dedication. It also requires the acquisition of knowledge and the development of an understanding about many things.

It is not new or arcane material that the Druid needs to acquire. Most of what a Druid comes to know and understand is familiar. Being drawn to a particular Way is a gradual and educative process, for all that any of us may suddenly realize that it has happened. Every Druid can look back as far as their early childhood and trace the influences that guided them on to and along the Way.

Familiar as aspects of knowledge and understanding may be, however, once committed to the Way, a Druid will learn about all things anew from the distinct perspective of the Celtic metaphysic. In so doing, they come to understand things more deeply, appreciating significances that were formerly obscured to them. They also learn that there is much they can and must discard - especially those ideas and behaviours we are forced into believing are necessary for the maintenance of the World.

In this manner, Druids re-explore the charted regions of their being, reshaping what they are. From there they are able to venture more widely, moving firstly into the uncharted territories of their selves. In this, they learn much that provides the strength, the knowledge, the understanding, and the wisdom to Serve.

A Druid will also re-explore the universe and come to know it from the new perspective of their evolving self, learning not just that they will Serve, but *how* they can Serve. The universe is, of course, a vast and complex place that exists on many levels. It is also extremely ancient, with all prospect that it will continue to exist for time out of mind. So it is a place in which it is very easy, even for the most astute, to get lost. As in the World, there is also much distraction. The universe, however, is far less dangerous than the World. It is just so much larger. That is why a sense of place, a sense of rootedness, is so important to all of us in the outer, material world of which we are so manifestly a part.

The place we truly are, a centre, home, the hearth, another person - all these are heart points from which we can take our bearings on our outward journeys of exploration. They are the beacons that guide our return.

The inner planes in which the Druid journeys are not, in material incarnation, the place of our home - no matter how welcome any of us may be there, no matter how much we may desire it to be so. There is no stable, physical point there on which to centre ourselves permanently. That is why we have guides to keep us oriented. That is why, when we extend our work in the universe to the dimension of time, it is done through the medium of our ancestors and with an eye to the responsibilities we have toward our descendants.

Coming to know and understand both the self and the universe, however, is not all there is to becoming Druid, even though these tasks or quests will have been approached from that specific perspective. As it stands, such knowledge and understanding - no matter how comprehensive, no matter how deep - lacks the special energy that inspires it with life.

Without a regard for life, the quest for knowing and understanding will be an interesting, but ultimately fruitless task. Empty. Without soul. And those who undertake it, if they take it no further than that, will always feel unfulfilled, bereft of the power to make right change in the World. And making change in the World is what Service, the very essence of the Druid Way, is all about. It is through that selfless application, a giving out of one's own vital force, that one achieves fulfilment.

So, what more must be done? Whence comes the necessary vital energy? What action is it that animates what we have come to know? How do we fill the emptiness? How engender the soul? The answer is simple. Connection - the act of unifying.

Of course, the application is nowhere near as simple as the answer. Reaching out openly, touching, forging links, maintaining and developing relationships, opening channels through which the primal energies of existence can flow to and through us - these are all complex processes that need sensitivity and patience. Nor can the energies involved simply be tapped and allowed to flow unchecked or unguided. They are far too powerful. In their raw form they would overwhelm and destroy us as surely as they would unbalance and harm the rest of creation.

In order to vitalize knowledge and understanding safely, release the power inherent in what has been learned, and channel it to right Service, a Druid must come to know and understand how they stand in relation to the universe. Knowing and understanding that, they must then become practised in that relation for all relations are dynamic and active just as the Druid Way itself is dynamic and active.

Coming to know and understand how we stand in relation to the universe is the most difficult of the many complex quests that face anyone who undertakes a commitment to the Druid Way. Not only do such investigations have no place in the normal scheme of things, making them alien to our way of thought and our way of dealing with life, but working with the basic energies of existence is also absent from everyday consideration.

Certain inbuilt assumptions, fundamental to the structure and maintenance of mundane society and the education system it spawns, inhibit our questioning its authority and questing beyond its strict material limits. Spiritual understanding and exploring our place in the universe are not things that come naturally to us as fields of academic or practical study. Indeed, we can all too easily assume that our relation to the universe, as well as our relationship with it, is something that just happens, sorting itself out as it goes along. As a result, the establishment, maintenance, and development of such relationships are all too often neglected. Yet friendships, love, they all need work.

We cannot afford to leave such an important aspect of our being unquestioned and unquested. We cannot afford to leave it to develop as chance and the base intent of others dictates because what we are depends on our relations with the rest of creation. We must play a fully informed part in that or else we become lost to ourselves.

There is a further danger to our sense of identity. In exploring and working with the universe, we find that it reaches into both space and time. Space is the more familiar of these and we work there with a degree of ease. It is the natural habitat of our material form. Time, however, for all that it is a dimension in which we naturally exist, is unfamiliar territory. Like the inner planes it is easier to negotiate if we have guides with whom we can identify - our ancestors and descendants. In establishing stronger connections and understanding of our relationship with both our ancestors and descendants, however, it is all too easy to lose touch with ourselves. We can lose not only the relationship we have with ourselves, but also the understanding we have of what our self is.

We lose touch because of the very thing we do. We work and explore to become Druid. As we do so, we evolve. The evolution is actually accelerated by the nature of our exploration. Indeed, our evolution is the whole point. And as we evolve, the universe evolves. The links we forge with the universe are, therefore, dynamic, changing, constantly forged anew. What each of us is now is different from what we were even a few months ago. For a Druid, exploring the great, vibrant forest of the Celtic metaphysic, the changes can be immense.

If we lose sight of our self and what we are constantly becoming, then we lose sight of the universe, we lose sight of our own essential being. For, in our relationship with the world, and in the flow of energies back and forth between our evolving self and the rest of the universe, is to be found the dynamic tension of our personal existence. This it is that stimulates being, drives evolution, kindles learning, increases understanding, and gives birth to joy. Through this perspective - that of the dynamic tension of our existence - brought alive in a specific way by our quest along the forest paths of the Druid Way, we come to know and understand our selves, the universe, and our place in it. We are also opened up to our pasts, our present, and our possible futures more clearly. And the more we search, the wider and brighter are the horizons we are enabled to explore, the more open we become to what we find.

In doing all this, we are also assisting others in their quest to know and understand their relation with the spatial and temporal world more clearly. Our existence, being dynamic and directed toward an understanding and right influence of the primal energies, resonates concordantly through both space and time. Making connections is an act of unification. It is precisely what the universe is and does. If we are also engaged in that act, we work with the universe, we cause fewer crosscurrents to upset the journey of others.

This assistance resonates through many dimensions and in many directions. Not only do we touch the lives of many others in whatever is our present incarnation, but we also each live many lives. We are the future to those in our past; we are the ancestors of those who are yet to be. So it is that we have an enormous responsibility to those that have been, to our present companions, and to those who will come after us (ourselves re-incarnate, after all). We have a responsibility to manage ourselves and our relationship with the universe not only in right fashion, but also with grace.

Grace can be a difficult concept to understand. The use of the word has been much polarized in recent centuries - torn in two directions by the linear dualism of modern materialistic thought. In common parlance, it has increasingly come to be associated with the outward, physical appearance of things - especially movement. In theological parlance, it is used in the sense of the condition of being favoured by deity. As such, it is seen by most folk as a different sort of grace - a purely spiritual phenomenon. To further complicate matters, grace is all too often seen as an end in itself, the reward for hard work, the goal achieved, the gift bestowed.

The dissociation of meaning, along with the notion that grace is a final cause, is demeaning in the extreme. Where grace is truly present it permeates the whole being. It is a divine influence operating in and through people who have touched the universe and been touched by it as lovers touch. And through these people this influence enters the World to regenerate and to sanctify. This can only work if grace is made manifest both materially and spiritually at one and the same time. If not, it is not truly grace. As such, it is not a goal, it is not an end. Indeed, in one sense it is merely a by-product of right action and right thought. Through these we open that channel to the divine, to the primal energies of being. It is that, passing through us in controlled form, which manifests as grace.

Right action *and* right thought. Action and thought are normally considered (when considered at all) to be entirely different orders of existence. These are the physical and the mental - and never shall the two quite connect (although it is allowed that thought, on occasion, may be causative of action). And so it has been held by many for at least the last three hundred years. Yet any careful examination of our manifest being will give the lie to such a notion. After all, if action and thought really were different orders of existence, then they could never connect and one could not, under any circumstances, cause the other. Nor could they coexist as aspects of our being as happily as they do.

Action and thought are not disparate. They are not even separate. On the contrary, although clearly distinct, they are correlative manifestations of unitary being. The ways in which we act are fundamental to the ways in which we think. The ways in which we think are equally fundamental to the ways in which we act. Action is the body's thought, as thinking is the mind's action. All are facets of a single being.

Furthermore, as manifestations of unitary being, action and thought do not occur aimlessly, working in different directions or at cross-purposes. Each derives from and works within a single, unifying framework that guides our being. Most of us remain unaware of what that guidance consists in, but it does exist. Indeed, much of it is directed towards our material manifestation. But just as thought and action are distinct expressions of a single being, so too are the material and the spiritual.

The framework shapes us, but it is not irredeemably rigid. It is a living thing and we can help to shape it by using it. And the more the framework is exercised, the more sophisticated it becomes. Action and thought stimulate the evolution of the framework. As it evolves, more and more sophisticated acts and thoughts can be and are derived from it. Doing *and* being, thought *and* action, therefore, are fundamental and unified aspects of the continuity and evolution of our being.

The basic framework is with us from an early stage of manifestation, in place and working by the time we are born. From that moment on it gives direction to our action and structure to our thinking. At first, these are all concerned with the basics of life. Learning in the early months and years of our lives goes forward at the most extraordinary pace and with enormous capacity - never to be matched again in that lifetime. By the time we are five years of age, all the hard work is done, all the basic skills are in place. By the time we are seven or eight, the advanced skills (should) have been acquired. In later years, we become concerned more with patterning what we learn, evolving more sophisticated models of what we understand of the world in which we exist.

Patterning takes up an increasing amount of physical and intellectual energy, directed toward creating an increasingly complex framework. As it increases in sophistication, it derives more and more from - and may eventually entirely consist in - the metaphysical stance or world view into which each of us is inducted from our birth. Such a stance, in turn, both colours and reinforces the ways in which we respond to the universe and the World, further reinforcing the patterns we make of our experience.

Metaphysical stances are rarely adopted consciously. They are even more rarely coherent and self-contained frameworks. We are not taught the skills necessary to make this so. The predominant metaphysic of our society actually prevents this. Most of the direction and structure of our thought and action are, therefore, initially derived from a framework that has been imposed upon us haphazardly without any real consideration of its coherence or consistency.

In most cases the metaphysic we grow up with is imposed upon us without our realisation - sometimes in order to ensure we conform. Mostly, however, it is imposed upon us by those who have thrived within it and who are, therefore, psychologically predisposed toward it. Indeed, a given metaphysic is usually so deeply inherent in, as well as fundamental to, the systems that deliver it (family, school, community, religious or spiritual tradition, and so on), we are all too often unaware that it represents anything other than the correct or only way of thinking. We may not even realize it exists at all - hence so much ideological conflict in the World.

All people alter their frameworks within what they see as acceptable norms as they go through life. Some come into conflict with these norms, in most cases without ever understanding where the conflict lies. Relatively few people actually break away from their inherited framework sufficiently to recognize it for what it is. Fewer still make the difficult and courageous decision to examine the metaphysic they hold and the way they behave. Even less take the further steps necessary to change themselves and their lives in accordance with the conclusions they reach. This final step is difficult enough when you consider the many external pressures there are on a person to conform to accepted standards. There is, however, a single, hidden pressure far greater than any of those imposed from outside. The self.

The single major reason it is so difficult to make such changes and adopt a coherent and self-contained metaphysic that is distinct from or even at odds with the one in which we were brought up, is that central to any metaphysic we adopt is the view we hold of our self. It is, after all, the self that holds, is shaped by, and acts upon that view. It may even be that the self and the metaphysic are synonymous.

However that may be, and whatever else the self consists in, it is extremely resistant to major change. When all else is said and done, if you work to change the self too much and too quickly, then the very basis of selfhood, identity, is threatened. So too is the relation of the self to itself and to the rest of the universe. Such change represents an extreme leap of faith and is best carried on under the watchful eye of a guide who can offer help if and when help is needed.

There are, of course, many aspects of the self, most of which have been explored and discussed in great depth elsewhere. Who we are and who we are to become is determined in part by genetics. But that is far from everything. Who we are is largely the result of ecological considerations, of the many and vastly differing environments in which we circulate. Genetics may set up the parameters within which we are and can be influenced, but without influence as a pressure to develop we would remain as day old babies and soon perish. There is, of course, a third element, working from within - the soul.

Of all the many environments in which we circulate, the single largest factor that influences the development of our personality is other people. We evolve and mature as persons by interacting with other people. We all do this in different ways and to different degrees, but it is people that shape people. Sadly, although people are important, interaction with them is now largely second-hand, and even that is all too often at the expense of interaction with other elements of our overall environment.

Too much emphasis on interaction with other people, especially the wrong kinds of interaction, distorts our view of the universe. We need also to interact with the wind and the rain, the sun and the stars, with city streets and sheep grazed meadows, with animals and with trees. It is something else that we are not taught how to do. Yet without these forms of connection and interaction - without a dialogue with the many facets of the universe accessible to us - we cannot possibly fulfil our potential as persons.

Despite the fact that many aspects of the self have been investigated in great depth, there is one aspect that receives scant attention but which is, nonetheless, of great importance in determining identity. An exploration and understanding of this aspect, as well as a change in our thought and action in respect of it, is a key to right change in many other ways. It unlocks our ability to construct our own, coherent metaphysic as well as enabling us to form better and more meaningful links with the universe.

The particular aspect of the self that is the key to so much else may seem simple and in some ways it is. In other ways it is extremely complex. Like a game that is easy to learn, but which takes a lifetime to realize. It is the distinction we learn to make between what is our self and what is not our self. Or, to pose it as a question in words of a more immediate nature, where and what is the boundary between me and not me?

One of the difficulties in answering this question lies in the fact that, in dealing with our self, we are not dealing with an exclusively material entity. We are psychological and spiritual beings as well. And the self is also, in part, an evolving complex of relationships. We are not, therefore, fixed beings. We change from day to day. We behave differently according to environment, respond differently to different persons and combinations of people. What is more, we learn from the way we behave and the responses we elicit. This is partly what one might term unconscious social training, but it also occurs on an increasingly conscious level as we mature - different facets of a person's nature waking and manifesting themselves.

Even with no people around, we constantly interact with whatever constitutes our environment and we behave and react according to the given circumstance. So, the complex of relationships that are instrumental in shaping the self involves the rest of the animate and the inanimate World as well as the universe. Indeed, everything within our purview - the totality of personal experience. And if this is so, we need to ask the question again, where does each of us stop and the rest of the universe begin?

To some this will sound trite. Yet the question is, quite literally, of vital importance. It is fundamental to the way in which we treat the planet, the universe, the World.

If you should answer with the accepted premiss that the self is contained within the epidermis and that the skin is the border beyond which the rest of the universe begins, you will immediately alienate yourself from everything else that exists. Stating that, you cannot, thereafter, truly claim to know anything about the universe or the World with any certainty. They become materially, aesthetically, spiritually, intellectually, emotionally, psychologically, and politically unknowable. They also become untouchable and closed to any influence you might wish to exert upon them.

By taking such a stance you could not even logically consider other people because you could only know and acknowledge the existence of your own self with any degree of certainty. And even that is uncertain. *Cogito ergo sum* has no meaning on which to build as it is a tautological statement. The inner life no longer has validity. Thus isolated, the vision one holds of one's self becomes, of necessity, synchronous and synonymous with the material body. That becomes the central, the only concern. The spirit withers. The self becomes truly selfish.

The absurdity of the idea that we are autonomous and fully contained within the skin is clear. Anyone adopting this model of the self (and many people do) will suffer great psychic, spiritual, psychological, and physiological distress. This is because it is an untenable position, no matter how much anyone may pretend otherwise. They cannot rely on the Cartesian tautology to demonstrate, assert, and maintain their being. They cannot stand in splendid isolation. This is because the self has to have interaction with the rest of the universe if only to survive, let alone flourish. Without interaction, psychoses set in and begin to govern both thought and action. This may seem to beg the question of whether or not the universe is an objective reality existing independently of our perception of it. It does not matter. Real in that sense or not, the rest of the universe is essential to the self.

Worse still than simply causing psychotic thought and behaviour, a metaphysic in which the universe is seen as separate from and wholly other than the self locks the person who holds it into a vicious circle. Their denial of the universe causes them distress. Distress will often manifest itself as denial. Yet the universe is there, as is the World, and they will not ignore a person, no matter how much the person may try and ignore them. And the more the universe attempts to break through into their isolation, the more that person reacts aggressively and attempts (subconsciously or otherwise) to destroy that which is so disturbing to them and their beliefs. Such destruction can be of the universe; it is more likely to be of the World. It will always be of the self.

There is, of course, another model of what the self is and where the border between it and the universe is to be found. It is a model, however, that requires us to accept a basic truth that is much rejected. That truth is that we interact in all ways and at all times with the universe in all its forms; that what we are is due, if only in part, to that interaction. Accepting that truth means also accepting that the self is not and cannot be contained within the epidermis. Rather, it extends beyond that to embrace all that we experience at any given moment in time.

All that we experience of the universe consists in our interaction with it. These interactions help to shape what we are. It is a shape that, as we have seen, constantly changes according to environment. A constant change of shape must also mean a constant change of boundary. This ever changing shape includes within its boundary other people, animals, plants, objects, places, landscapes, machines, ideas, dreams, stars, and so on. This is not to say the self is *only* these interactions. All these things must have something with which to interact. There is, of course, a physical body (although even that changes constantly), but there is also an essential and evolving soul, a quintessential spark that is the self and only knowable to the self.

If during normal, everyday life our self engages with, enfolds, takes form from, and is shaped to greater or lesser degree by all that we interact with and experience, then our self is inseparable from the universe. All the people, plants, places, animals, stars, dreams, and so on that we interact with are a very real part of us. What we are, in part, is what they are. The self, therefore, includes all those things as and when we have contact with them. And not just as sense impressions.

So, if you walk in a forest, for example, everything that you experience there shapes you - in direct relation to the impression it makes upon you. Whilst you are there, the forest is physically, aesthetically, spiritually, emotionally, intellectually, part of yourself. Equally, your self is part of the forest in the same way. And when you leave the forest it remains part of your self, just as part of yourself remains with the forest.

The forest will have changed you in some fashion just as you will have changed it. Our self, therefore, moves through life expanding and contracting in a vital dance in which the essential self lives its own evolving life distinct but never separate from the rest of the universe. We are all part of one another, part of every creature, part of every star, part of every stone, part of all that is. And all that is, becomes part of us.

This way of viewing the universe has many responsibilities. If we accept it, we must live as if we accept it. Harm any part of the universe and, sooner or later, we harm ourselves. We cannot avoid changing the universe as we pass through. That is what living creatures and dynamic systems do. That is what they are. It is also a function of Service - an essential of the Druid Way. Service, however, is qualified by being limited to right action and right change. In recognizing that we are integral to the universe, we should work to make our passage through it a gentle one, if only to minimize the harm we do to our self. This is not being selfish, but self-interested. That, within this metaphysic, is synonymous with becoming interested in others and, through the many overlapping fields of being that we consist in, the whole of the planet, the whole of creation.

There is a great deal more to explore here, especially in relation to the relative power of things to affect the self as well as the nature of the change effected. When a thing becomes a part of you, it changes your whole being irrevocably. Nothing is ever just tacked on to be discarded at will. All change is organic. All change is holistic. A thing absorbed alters the whole system so that a new whole (not dissimilar to the last) comes into being. It is a constant evolution.

For all that, it is not simply a case of taking things in, it is also that the core of one's self reacts, becomes more sophisticated, gains a better understanding of the universe, the self, and the relationship between the two. Every meal you eat, every conversation you have, every dream you dream, every book you read, every hand you hold, every hole you dig and tree you plant - alters you, shapes you, becomes you. The thing that does not help to make you what you are does not exist. The whole universe constantly flows through you and becomes you - you flow constantly back out and become as one with it.

In this we can all find identity. Not only in the sense of knowing more clearly who we are, but also in that of finding communion. This metaphysic, that of our Celtic ancestors, is the basis of the Druid Way and informs all that a Druid does and is. It is what we must all learn to encompass; it is from where we must all begin. Reaching forward and outward on a great quest so that we might, one day, find we have gone full circle.

TO WHERE THE JOURNEY RETURNS

The future. That which is to be. It is in our hands to shape it as we will, but we should take care to know where it truly lies. For the future is not 'out there' - beyond our grasp, forward in time; it is 'in here' - within the soul, the heart, the spirit, the mind. Without changes on the inside, without a radical re-alignment of ideas, without a new perspective, without a re-patterning, there will be none of us left to shape any kind of future at all. Human beings will have turned in to an evolutionary dead-end and become human havings - driven there by a destructive greed.

It is the future we wish to shape that should direct our actions, based on a wisdom derived from and moulded by a thorough understanding of the past. Yet we cannot let either the past or the future direct everything we do and think, any more than we should allow other people to do that. The consequences of such folly are all too apparent in the World today.

No matter how important tomorrow may be, we always live at the time we live in and not at some other time. The 'now' is when we must exist, when we must work toward a unified existence, when we must do and improve and learn so that there is a continuity of these things. The future is made today, within the very heart of each of us.

It is not the universe we are trying to change, for that would be futile and dangerous - to limb, life, and spirit. It is the spirit, the soul, which each Druid works to change that it might move and work rightly in the universe as it is, not as we would wish it to be. The World is a different matter. That we *can* change, and must, although we cannot do it by being a part of that which sustains it.

It takes much courage, but if we truly care for the planet, for what exists beyond the World, we must step beyond the narrow limits of the predominant metaphysic and find a new Way. Those who are Druid have done just that - they have started their journeys, they began from where they were, they face that which is to be, working gently in the now to heal and to re-balance.

For those still wondering, still contemplating the journey, I hope the foregoing has cast some Light.

Take courage.

Make the leap.